MEN CAN

MEN CAN

The Changing Image
and Reality of Fatherhood
in America

Donald N. S. Unger

TEMPLE UNIVERSITY PRESS PHILADELPHIA

TEMPLE UNIVERSITY PRESS
Philadelphia, Pennsylvania 19122
www.temple.edu/tempress

Library of Congress Cataloging-in-Publication Data

Unger, Donald N. S. (Donald Nathan Stone)
  Men can : the changing image and reality of fatherhood in America /
Donald N. S. Unger.
    p.   cm.
  Includes bibliographical references and index.
  ISBN 978-1-4399-0000-0 (hardcover : alk. paper)   1. Fatherhood—
United States.   2. Fathers—United States.   3. Parenting—United States.
4. Father and child—United States.   I. Title.
  HQ756.U54 2010
  306.874'20973—dc22   2009048500

Printed in the United States of America

2 4 6 8 9 7 5 3 1

To the memory of my grandmother

Rebecca Unger,

who made this and most other things possible.

And to her namesake,

my daughter, **Rebecca**,

who made it necessary.

Contents

· · · · · · · · ·

Acknowledgments

. . . .

Acknowledgments are chiefly made up of a public recitation of what was done to make a book possible. This book had its genesis in the dissertation I completed for my doctorate from the University of Massachusetts at Amherst in 2001. I'll get to that in a moment. But I want to start somewhat backwards: with the master's of fine arts in fiction that I earned from the University of Michigan in 1990 and with something crucially *not* done.

In the earliest conversations that I had with fellow students at Michigan, we quickly picked out some common experiences: everyone immediately understood when you talked about lying in bed late at night and into the small hours of the morning, trying to sleep, trying *not* to get out of bed, trying *not* to write, and eventually finding that the only way to get rest was to give in to the words that *needed* to be released from your head—writing as excretion, writing as therapy.

Everyone also had a story—usually more than one—about the friends and family members who had asked them when they were going to "get a real job."

Not in my family.

Not in my family, not in my wife's family, not among any of the people that I consider family by choice if not by blood or marriage.

More than anything else, to be a writer, to be any kind of artist—and, putting aside the fiction and poetry I've published, I'll stand behind the idea of scholarly writing as having an important artistic component to it—is an arrogant (and tenuous) act of assertion.

I am officially credentialed in a variety of ways—as a teacher, as a driver, as the operator of a nail gun and a core drill. No degree, license, or certificate I have ever earned, however, really made me a writer. That's something you have to do for yourself, but it's something you can't do alone.

What gave me the time and space to become a writer—even before the matter of active support, even before the matter of mentoring and practice—was the forbearance of friends and family: you're a thin-skinned balloon as any kind of artist; everyone kept their pins to themselves.

That's not a small thing. That's not something I have *ever* taken for granted.

Anne Herrington, my dissertation director at the University of Massachusetts at Amherst, was crucial in making the first iteration of this project possible. She was supportive and encouraging; she was critical in the best meaning of that word. She was respectful of my intentions and concerns; she was adamant about standards.

Charlie Moran, who was on both the dissertation committee and the qualifying exam committee before that, was a pleasure to work with for the entire time I was at the University of Massachusetts: always enthusiastic, always serious, always demanding clarity and concision.

Deborah Carlin and Jean Nienkamp, who served on the qualifying exam committee, and Pat Griffin, of the University of Massachusetts School of Education, who served on my dissertation committee, were all consistently generous with their time, available, serious, supportive, and helpful.

I have been extremely lucky, in that all of the people I worked with—at the University of Massachusetts and elsewhere—were very clear about the line between their obligation to make sure that what

I wrote adhered to the standards and achieved the professional purpose(s) necessary at various stages and the ego issue of whose work this was.

I never had the slightest doubt that any counsel I was given, whether I agreed with it or not, was given with the goal of making my work better.

That's not something I have ever taken for granted either—a tough line to walk as a teacher, an example I have tried to follow with my own students.

The families who were gracious enough to open their lives to me, whose stories I have endeavored to tell—those named and those who preferred the cloak of anonymity—did a brave and difficult thing. I have tried to depict them accurately and fairly, tried not to bend or distort their stories. I am grateful for what they were willing to share with me; without their cooperation, this book would not have been possible. I admire as well the various ways in which they approach parenting; they have taught me a lot.

You worry about your parents sometimes when they are younger, but mine have grown up to be fine people. My father, Stephen Unger, and my mother, Marion Baker, have matured a lot over the years, and that's been a pleasure to watch (and to benefit from). My aunt and uncle, Muriel and Paul Krell, have been unstinting in their emotional support since the day I was born. I have sometimes referred to them, only half in jest, as "The Patron Saints of Office Equipment." You need time and space to write, but you also need tools, and they have always been generous in providing them.

Mick Gusinde-Duffy, my editor at Temple University Press, fought for and stood behind this book, gave sage counsel and sympathetic support, and helped provide additional framework but was respectful of how I wanted to do things—I hear he's a good father too, and that doesn't surprise me at all.

Finally, I started working on this project because of my daughter, Rebecca; I could never have finished it without a plethora of supports from my wife, Cynthia. They are, together, the best things that ever happened to me.

I went back to school to get my doctorate when Rebecca was two and a half years old; there was no way to disentangle what was going on in my family life from what was going on in my professional and academic life. I wasn't interested in trying.

Anne Lamott has said that we write from our wounds. In the book *Bird by Bird* she tells her readers, "In this dark and wounded society, writing can give you the pleasures of the woodpecker, of hollowing out a hole in a tree where you can build your nest and say, 'This is my niche, this is where I live now, this is where I belong'" ([New York: Pantheon, 1994], 234).

I've always felt that the scholarly corollary to Lamott is "We theorize from our irritations." Academic and theoretical questions hold little interest to me if they are unmoored from the urgency of our everyday lives.

To my way of thinking, *What is going on here? Why is this happening?* and *What can we do to change this?* all make fine writing prompts.

I love my daughter because she's my daughter; I love her writing because she is a fine writer. She finished writing her first novel when she was twelve; I see a groaning shelf of published books in her future. I'll be happy and proud to see her surpass me.

My wife has been an exceptional partner, exacting but flexible, honest but sensitive, intellectual but warm. A fine scholar herself, she has long borne the often thankless task of first-line reader: she gives nuanced, perceptive feedback; I go off to sulk for a while. Virtually none of the puzzle pieces of my life—personal, professional, parental—would work without her; certainly I never could have finished the many drafts and versions of this book.

I thank you all.

Introduction:
When You Comin'
Home, Dad?

· · · · · · · ·

It was a Sunday night and my daughter, Rebecca, and I were heading north on the Merritt Parkway, through Connecticut, back home to Massachusetts, after a weekend of visiting friends and family in and around New York City. On the radio a father was singing a lament about having missed his son's childhood—you know the song.

Rebecca was eight at the time, and I was in the middle of two years of teaching as a visiting professor in the English Department at the University at Albany, some hundred and forty miles from where we lived—a five-hour commute, round trip (though for the most part I had to do it only twice a week). Any time I told people where I was teaching and where I lived, they asked if—or sometimes simply assumed that—I was living in Albany half the week. It was a question that always irritated me. Would they make the same assumption about a *mother* with a young daughter?

I'd turned the song up and told Rebecca to listen to it closely. When it was over, I asked her what she thought it was about.

This Introduction is adapted, in part, from an essay in Shira Tarrant, ed., *Men Speak Out: Views on Gender, Sex, and Power* (New York: Routledge, 2008).

"That the father is sad he didn't see his son grow up?" Rebecca asked, only a little tentatively.

"That's right," I told her, proud, like any parent, that my daughter could intelligently analyze and answer questions—even if I was the only one there to hear what she had to say.

Rebecca paused.

Then she said, "That's why you don't have an apartment in Albany, right? Because you don't want to be like the man in the song."

"That's right," I said again, working on keeping the emotion out of my voice, concentrating on the road ahead of me.

"I'm glad," Rebecca said.

"Me too."

"Did you get the idea from the song?" she asked me.

"No," I told her.

That my daughter is good at analyzing song lyrics and other texts, that she was good at this from a very young age, makes sense: I teach writing; my wife teaches Spanish language, literature, and film; many of our friends and family members on both sides are academics as well. That she would be particularly keyed in to what amount to issues of parenting, gender, and division of domestic labor makes sense too.

I've been talking, writing, and not uncharacteristically complaining about these issues since before my daughter's birth, in 1995—back into my own childhood, really, but I'll get to that.

It also makes sense that we were having that conversation in the car; that's where a good deal of modern-day parent-child relating takes place. And, from the time Rebecca was weaned, at eighteen months, while I was in the midst of a couple of years of being the stay-at-home parent and my wife was working days, nights, weekends, and holidays—doing whatever was necessary to earn her tenure—my daughter and I also regularly drove that route to and from New York City; these topics came up more often than one might think they would.

When Rebecca was three and a half—with the pro bono assistance of Deborah Ellis, a professor of law at New York University and former legal counsel for the National Organization for Women's Legal Defense Fund[1]—I got the Mobil Oil Corporation to comply with state law in Connecticut and in New York State and install changing tables in the men's rooms in the rest stops along Route 15, which encompasses the Wilbur Cross, the Merritt, and the Hutchinson River parkways. It's worth noting that federal law offers no cause of action in such a situation. Achieving gender equity in college athletics is a federal matter— with which I have no quarrel. Whether fathers can change their children's diapers indoors while traveling, however, is a "state's rights" matter with which the federal government chooses not to trifle.

For months afterward, any time I took Rebecca into a men's bathroom, she would look around and then ask me, "Are you going to make them put a changing table in here too?"

I would if I could, and I know I'm not alone in holding that view.

Professor Ellis had a running start in taking on Mobil on my behalf: A few years earlier, her husband, also an attorney, had taken similar action against the Lord & Taylor department store chain for its failure to have changing tables in men's rooms.

He won too.

It may be that the tide is beginning to turn in terms of how we see fathers and how fathers see themselves, in how we talk about parenting, and in how we represent parents in the media, in popular art, in everyday language.

As far as I'm concerned, those changes can't come fast enough; I've been waiting for them almost all of my life.

You Say You Want a Revolution? Well, Y' Know . . .

The gender messages being broadcast in the 1970s, when I was an adolescent, were decidedly mixed. On the one hand, the feminist movement was a force to be reckoned with. Women and men who wanted change—both full civil and economic rights for women and a more comprehensive fracturing of gender roles overall—were visible, vocal, and, in many ways, ascendant. The Equal Rights Amendment was working its way through state legislatures; many people thought it was on its inevitable way to ratification.

As a teenage boy who did babysitting in addition to mowing lawns and washing cars, these issues were directly relevant to me, not simply matters of intellectual interest. It was hard not to wonder exactly what was going on.

There were people happy to see a boy taking care of children. Still, when I was the male voice on the phone, *claiming* to be the babysitter, I seemed to panic the occasional grandparent or friend of the family when they called: Now and then, I was quizzed on difficult questions like the child's name—as if I might have been a slightly dim home invader who had yet to learn that it was poor form to pick up the phone mid-rampage.

My family circumstances also made these issues more concrete than abstract. My mother was a Zionist socialist who left New York City for Israel on graduating high school, shortly after the declaration of statehood. In part, she said in later years, she was looking for a living arrangement that dispensed with a good deal of the traditional, gendered division of labor. A few years of living on a kibbutz—I picture her, more or less self-described, making a huge cauldron of soup, stirring it with a canoe paddle—convinced her that Israel was not to be the home of this then-radical alternative. She returned to New York and took a job as a public health nurse.

My grandmother and my aunt on my father's side of the family were also both strong and crucial presences for me: women with as much intellectual and philosophical force to them as emotional intensity.

My parents divorced when I was in my early teens, and my younger sister and I stayed with my father. I remember the theory that we were each to make dinner two nights per week; I don't remember clearly how cleaning chores were divided up—although I have some dim memory of charts. This system did not work smoothly or easily, but I don't believe we were undernourished. And—if the house was somewhat dingy, and at times in disarray—I don't recall filth at the level of health hazard. No one was ever hired to come in and cook or clean during that period of time, so we must have somehow done it ourselves, with my father actively participating, as well as playing the crucial supervisory role.

In the larger society, during the same period, while there was some intense cultural and political battling going on—backlash even then, early and fierce—there was also genuine and growing support for women to take on "nontraditional" work roles, which at that time still meant almost any role outside of secretarial work, teaching in elementary school, or nursing.

On the broader domestic front, both images and realities were beginning to change as well—in part as a result of increased workforce participation on the part of women. Popular culture began to provide intermittent glimpses of men doing housework, cooking, and taking care of children, like an analogue broadcast television station at the edge of the signal, flickering through the interference. But those changes—it seemed to me then and I've found no reason to change my view in retrospect—were *at least* as controversial as women moving into the workplace in increasing numbers, if not more so.

John Irving's novel *The World According to Garp* came out in 1978, when I was in high school. The title character was a writer, a stay-at-home father, and a great cook. Sounded cool to me. But to a lot of people *Garp* seemed to be more wacky than admirable, more literary magic than realistic option.

John Lennon was holed up in the Dakota, on Manhattan's Upper West Side—a few blocks from where my mother lived—having essentially given up making music to bake bread and take care of his son Sean. Some people saw this as a positive model; I certainly did. But others interpreted the way that he was living his life as just another way in which he had been emasculated by Yoko Ono—ugly strains of misogyny and racism (she was a Dragon Lady, in this view, who first broke up the Beatles and then broke John's spirit). How else to explain his choice to care for his son rather than continue his career? How else to explain the famous photo of Yoko, lying down, clothed in black, John curled against her, naked and fetal?

On television, there were commercials that depicted men engaged in domestic labor. But I am hard pressed to remember any that showed this in an unalloyed, positive light. For the most part, in my memory, these commercials boil down to a set-piece exchange that is only slightly exaggerated.

OPEN ON:

Wide shot. Suburban household. Day. An inept father is standing in the kitchen, the sink piled high with dirty dishes, something burning on the stove, a two-foot dike of detergent foam leading the way to the clothes washer, around the corner, in the laundry room.

Father (*yelling to his wife, offscreen*): Honey, is it all right if I dry the kids in the microwave?

CUT TO:

Close up. Suburban household. Day. Wife's face as she surveys the mess from the kitchen doorway. A mixture of amusement and disdain at his incompetence clouds her features before she moves in to displace him and restore order.

Popular culture critic Mark Crispin Miller has dubbed these sorts of scenarios examples of "pseudo-feminism."[2] A focus on male domestic incompetence gives a surface appearance of recognizing the power and authority of women. But one doesn't have to read too deeply into the subtext to see that the message is neither liberatory nor egalitarian.

What conclusion could one draw from such a scene, other than that it would be sheer madness to "allow" men to continue to contribute to—*to take over!*—cooking, cleaning, or child care? It implies a willingness on the part of men to do such work but quickly demonstrates that we are simply not up to the task.

We bow to your superior skills . . . Now back to the kitchen, Honey.

What much of this suggests is that I *shouldn't* have been so quick to dismiss Rebecca's question about whether or not my behavior was cued or shaped by the song on the car radio. It's a song I grew up listening to; I remember, as well, the point in my childhood when part of the chorus of Pete Seeger's "Hammer Song" morphed from "all of my brothers" to "my brothers and my sisters," a change I found jarring—change isn't always smooth and even radical kids can evince a kind of "that's-not-how-I-learned-this" conservatism—but came to like. And of course—in addition to family, economics, politics, and a whole knot of other influences—books, movies, music, advertising, television, language, American culture both high and low, *did* do a lot to shape my ideas about what kind of parent a man should or could be.

How could they not have?

Where Are We Now?

I am writing neither as a social scientist nor as a demographer. It is not that I completely reject the descriptive power of numbers: A hydrogen atom consists of a single electron orbiting a single proton; that's not a matter up for discussion. But in describing social, cultural, or political trends, I believe numbers have limited utility.

They also have close to unlimited plasticity. More often than not, in examining social trends of any complexity, any good statistician can make the numbers dance. Statistics don't even stand still when we analyze them in retrospect.

In looking to generate statistics about domestic labor, moreover, how do we take measurements, and whose metrics do we find credible? Most of our information comes from survey data and from interviews. When a man says that he is doing X hours of labor taking care of his children on a weekly basis, what do we do when his wife says that he is actually doing ten hours less?

What *counts* as labor in this area? If a man says he took his kids to the park for three hours, giving his wife "time off," what do we do with her contention "Sure, he took them—after I spent an hour getting them ready, couldn't work while they were gone because I worried about him not being careful enough on the playground, and then spent another hour cleaning them up and settling them down once he brought them home!"

Are they both credited with three hours of child care in that situation?

Can she sustain a claim that this was actually five hours of child care on her part, compared to his three? Depends on what you believe, on who spins the story and how.

If I were simply to report the number of hours above in one configuration or another—three for him and none for her; three for him and five for her—that might give the appearance of good, quantitative solidity. But those numbers would do more to *hide* the truth than to reveal it. We learn more if we see the whole vignette: what happened, how the husband described it, how the wife described it—how the children saw the situation, if they were old enough to comment meaningfully.[3]

I am more interested, in the pages that follow, in narrative, in both weaving and examining the threads in credible *stories,* than I am in statistics. What we believe to be true, the personal—and cultural, and national—narratives to which we subscribe are powerful shapers of day-to-day reality.

My intention is for this book to act as a clarifying lens, focused on both American families (our friends, our neighbors, our co-workers) and on American culture (our language, our movies, our television programs, our advertising). My belief is that the landscape of the past few decades reveals, at bare minimum, the beginning of real change in how we take care of our children, in how we structure our households, in how we divide up domestic labor.[4] My hope is that exploring these issues and images will spark both recognition in readers and additional change in this direction.

When we examine change, of necessity, we look at why things often *don't* change, as well. I am particularly interested in the not uncommon resistance to the notion that much of anything has meaningfully changed around the quantity and the quality of the time American fathers spend with their children. Ironically, I see this resistance coming from both the right and the left.

Resistance on the right is easier to explain philosophically. Both men and women in more politically or culturally conservative families are apt to have a traditional view of gender: men are the breadwinners; women stay home and take care of the children.

To publicly *admit* to sharing domestic labor would amount to an admission of emasculation on two counts for the husband: for his failure to earn sufficient money "as he should" to permit his wife to stay home with the children and for his own taking up of "women's work." For the wife, it would amount to a public admission of *her* failure to take care of home and children "as she should" and her inappropriate usurpation of the prerogatives of the "proper head of the household."

Women work outside the home. That's no less true in conservative families than in progressive families. The economic pressures are the same; the economic lifeline—a second salary—is the same.

What *is* often different is what happens with child care and, of particular importance to what I am arguing, how this matter is discussed publicly. We have a national ambivalence about preschool day care, but this is closer to hardcore resistance in blue-collar or lower-middle-class conservative households. Day care, entrusting one's children to strangers—the financial costs aside—is more often viewed by such families as a shamefully unacceptable betrayal of family values and a potential venue for exposing children to a variety of dangers, both cultural and physical.[5]

As a result, evidence shows a large and vastly underreported increase in the number of conservative households in which men and women are sharing parenting to some degree, as a matter of necessity, both real and perceived. Most often this is true in families where both parents do shift work: nurses, utility workers,[6] police officers, firefighters.[7]

On the left, I believe there is resistance to acknowledging progress, in part, for fear that doing so will blunt the drive for further and more comprehensive change. I understand that concern; it is not my contention that we have reached some sort of postgender, egalitarian Promised Land where all are "Free to Be You and Me,"[8] but it is simply counterfactual to claim that we have not made substantial progress toward equality, along a variety of axes, in the past thirty-five years or so.

This resistance, which I would characterize as essentially tactical, is buttressed by an emotional reaction—on the part of at least some women and men of egalitarian bent—that might be summed up as follows:

"You want me to listen to *men's* problems and complaints now? *Puh-lease!*"[9]

In Chapter 6, for example, as part of an examination of the cultural impact of the 1979 movie *Kramer vs. Kramer*, I cite *New York Times* film critic Molly Haskell. Writing three years after the movie's release, she is both irritated by and dismissive of the movie in significant part because of this perceived inequity. "The supreme irony of *Kramer vs. Kramer*," she fumes, "was that here at last was a film that took on the crisis central to the modern woman's life, that is, the three-ring circus of having to hold down a job, bring up a child and manage a house simultaneously, and who gets the role? Dustin Hoffman."[10]

I understand the emotion; I understand its basis. But I don't believe that what she wrote was "useful," either to fathers or to mothers.

A medical analogy might help illuminate this.

In the 1980s, AIDS activists began to reshape medical care, from the drug testing and approval process, to hospital visiting regulations, to end-of-life care. AIDS was then almost exclusively a terminal illness; the patients were, as a group, younger than most other people in that situation, sometimes radical to begin with, sometimes radicalized by their experience with the illness; they fought to change the terms of their treatment and the terms of their deaths.

Some cancer patients and their families resented the changes the AIDS patients and their allies were able to initiate. *Why should* they *get privileged access to drugs still in clinical trials? Why should* they *have liberalized visiting policies? What gives* them *the right to challenge their physicians when the culture of medical care says we can't challenge ours?*

Some of those plaints—not often voiced publicly—were doubtless colored by homophobia. But they embody an obvious and powerful emotional logic untainted by that consideration: *I'm dying too! Don't I deserve the same attention?*

Ultimately, that's the narrative that won out, not a competition, not a zero-sum game in which the gains of one set of patients were construed to be the losses of another: The AIDS patients' rights movement birthed a *broader* patients' rights movement, rather than remaining at the level of "sectarian warfare" between patients suffering from different illnesses.[11]

Attention to the issues around fathers—married or divorced; custodial or noncustodial; working as primary parents, sharing child care, or working outside the home—should not be taken to be competition for attention to the issues faced by mothers. Indeed, while there may be some short-term, emotional benefit to guarding the territory of child care as a "women's issue," doing so also contributes to the ongoing marginalization of what I would instead call "parents' issues" in our political discourse.[12]

I understand Haskell's irritation. She brings up an issue, and an irony, that bears discussion. To launch that discussion as a public attack, however, amounts to parents arranging themselves in a circular firing squad.

Sometimes gender matters. Sometimes mothers and fathers have different concerns in terms of what makes our home lives or our professional lives either easier or more difficult (men don't get pregnant, for example). More often, however, our concerns overlap: We are more powerful when we stand together as parents than when we set ourselves up as fathers against mothers or vice versa.

So where are we now?

We may be on the cusp of fundamentally—and to my mind positively—shifting to a much more open definition of family and of caregiving generally, opening up and broadening what it is possible, or perhaps more accurately what it is *acceptable,* for a man to do with his life. A shorthand way of looking at this would be that in the next decade we may see the home open up to men in the same way that the workplace began to open up to women in the 1970s. I believe this would be good for men, for women, for children, though I would never assume that change is always easy or that it is ever neat.

On the other hand . . .

Perhaps instead we will see the reestablishment of much more rigid traditional gender roles: Men go out into the world to work; women tend home, hearth, and children.

In the pages that follow, I tell the story of American families in broad strokes and of a handful of fathers in some detail, of where we are and how we got here. I do this in two ways: by looking at families in which the father is either a stay-at-home parent or a co-parent and by examining how our image of (and as) fathers has changed over the past thirty-five years or so, the kind of language we use around parenting, the way we see fathers represented in movies, on television, in advertising.

Of the five families I profile, I have or had some connection to three of them: one is the family of one of my oldest and closest friends; two are families I met because they had children in the school my daughter attended from kindergarten through sixth grade.

I chose them because they represent a range of situations and motivations: how and why they have divided up child care is different from family to family; they live in different parts of the country; they are a reasonably ethnically diverse group of families. There were more than a dozen other families I considered but rejected.

I sought out the families whose stories bracket the book, at the beginning and at the end, because, in both cases, their situations were evocative of groundbreaking changes: the first because Ángel Nieto was a stay-at-home father in the 1970s, when this was an exceedingly rare role—and the fact of his son-in-law following in his footsteps is an interesting additional development; the last because the child-care-related gender discrimination case of former Maryland state trooper Kevin Knussman, in the 1990s, made news all the way up to the White House. The Knussmans, moreover, a religious family with strong conservative beliefs, also do something to illustrate the demographic in which I believe growth in shared care both has been underreported in the past and may provide a surprising source of change in the future.

Where possible, I interviewed the children as well as the adults. The impact that the changes regarding *who does what*—at home in general and with kids in specific—have on the "objects of our attention" and affection is key.

As to the cultural artifacts I have chosen to analyze—the movies, television programs, and advertisements—they are meaningful to *me*; I make here no grand claims about their absolute and irrefutable meaning or their statistical significance. I do believe, however, that viewed in context, these changing images of fathers and families both concretize and give more texture and color to evolving social trends than would a few pages of dry, quantitative analysis backed by "solid" numbers.

The *Ideal* Family?

If America is an ocean liner, we can think of families as individual cabins. It's not really my business what goes on in the other cabins, for the most part. We set the bar fairly high for the point at which the other families begin first knocking on and then, if necessary, knocking down your cabin door.

If it seems pretty clear that someone's getting hurt in there, we're coming in; that's a moral imperative. And if something going on in there seriously impacts the rest of us, that's going to bring us in as well. Your kids can't bore holes in the hull.

I don't care if it's a science project; my feet are getting wet and the buffet is beginning to list to starboard!

So, for starters, from my point of view, the members of the ideal family aren't hurting each other, and they aren't hurting the larger society. The ideal family is *functional*. For the most part, if it works, it's fine by me.

I'm not arguing for absolute parity in domestic labor. I'm not arguing for the superiority of "at home" parenting, however divided or configured, versus paid child care. I have something of a bias in favor of "more is better" when it comes to the number of adults, of whatever ages or genders, in the parental role, but I know plenty of loving and effective single parents—my own father among them, for a chunk of my childhood.

What I *am* arguing for more than anything is a greater openness to choice. I believe this would have a positive effect on parents, on children, on families. I would like to see this greater openness in society at large, within families, on the part of individuals.

Of course, one of the minefields one has to cross, in any discussion of gender roles, is the Nature-versus-Nurture debate. Here's where I stand:

It was clear as soon as our daughter was old enough to navigate the playground that I was willing to allow her to take greater physical risks than was my wife. Children periodically fall down, and I don't think that's always bad. In many ways, it's an important learning tool, far more effective than any safety lecture that I could give.

I wasn't being callous or indifferent when I gave Rebecca a bit more freedom. I didn't walk away from her when she was attempting something new and difficult, but when she was a toddler on the playground my hand was more likely to be six inches away from her; my wife more often remained in direct contact.

I've never felt that we had any meaningful philosophical difference there. I don't complain that my wife is smothering Rebecca; my wife doesn't accuse me of neglect. But our "emotional approach" is clearly slightly different, and that shapes who we are as parents. Go to almost any playground in America, and that's a statistically significant split, most often along gender lines.

One response is to ascribe this split to nurture rather than nature, an artifact of culture, a characteristic we can change—or that we're more confident about being able to change than we would be if we thought these tendencies were "wired," inborn gender differences.

I don't have the larger answer. Again, what I want to advocate for instead is respect for personal choice and individual difference. That doesn't resolve the larger question, but it isn't clear to me that the larger question *can* ultimately be resolved.

If geneticists find a variety of genes that they have been hunting for some time now—the genius gene, the criminal gene, the gay gene, the mothering gene, the super-athlete gene, the warrior gene—will this really put a smooth end to a variety of ideological and sociological debates that have been roiling societies for generations?

It seems unlikely.

We do better to look at actions in context and judge them apart from labels, to look at what is being done, rather than who is doing it. In observing a parent on a playground, then, the question becomes not "Is that child being maternally smothered or paternally neglected?" but rather "Does the level of attention being accorded the child fall within what we might describe as 'reasonable parenting practice'?"

Is that person taking care of the child?

Not a perfect solution.

It loses some of the warmth and specificity of either "maternal" or "paternal," has a slight tinge of the language of Socialist Realist theater to it:

Observe that Comrade Don is well within reasonable parenting practice in his attention to his child. Our congratulations, Comrade Don!

But it should be pointed out that this is essentially what women have been fighting for in the professional sphere for forty years or more: Judge me on how I do my job, not on whether or not I'm "a pretty good manager *for a woman*."

It is inevitable that our solutions will always be less than perfect. That doesn't mean we shouldn't keep pursuing improvement.

1

Ángel Nieto: The Leading Edge of Change

When I went back to Spain with my daughters and my wife, people there were amazed. They saw me with my daughter on my back and they couldn't believe it. For them it was shocking to see this change of roles.

—ÁNGEL NIETO

I'm sitting in Sonia Nieto's kitchen, in the home she shares with her husband, Ángel, and their twelve-year-old granddaughter, near the University of Massachusetts at Amherst, where Sonia teaches in the School of Education. It is a clean, spacious room: tile, exposed wood, lots of natural light. The rest of the downstairs is much the same: uncluttered but with most of the walls lined with bookshelves—plants distributed throughout. Sonia is in her early sixties. Her hair, mostly white, is short and stylishly cut, her eyes dark, her cheekbones high, her face mostly unlined. She's talking about her grandson, Celsito, her voice soft but clear and modulating musically, her hands animated.

"I had half an hour between something in Amherst and something in Northampton," she says, "so I drove through South Hadley to see them, because I love to see them, and there's Alicia [her daughter] feeding the four-month-old; Clarita, the eighteen-month-old, [is] sitting in the high chair, next to my daughter in the living room; and then I hear *'Alala! Alala!'*—which is what the kids call me—and there's little Celsito, my grandson, who's four, calling me into the kitchen. He's sitting on a stool, cutting up mushrooms, and helping his father cook."

"I said, '*¿Qué haces?*'" [What are you doing?], she continues. "He said, '*Estoy ayudando a papá a cocinar*'" [I'm helping Daddy cook].

"I was *astounded*," Sonia says, both her voice and her eyebrows rising. "Celso, my son-in-law, is so different from Ángel, *so, so* different—temperamentally, politically—and I thought, '*Celso has become Ángel!*' No matter what your politics are, you nurture your kids; you take care of your kids; you see it as part of your responsibility."

"When Celsito comes here," Sonia continues, "Ángel sits him up on the stool, and they make *madalenas* [madeleines] together."

She's not saying Celsito got the cooking bug from his grandfather, she hastens to add. Her son-in-law (Celso, Celsito's father) loves to cook too.

"Celso is very nurturing," she says. "He's a wonderful father. He's doing this stuff that I don't think his father would ever have dreamed of doing."

But that picture—three generations, all male, from grandson to grandfather, at ease in the kitchen, doing what would have been called "women's work" not long ago—makes Sonia just shake her head and smile.

"I think that things are really changing," she says.

That we are responsible for our families, of course, is an ancient idea. But what we *mean* by "responsible" changes, is largely a matter of time, of place, of culture, and—perhaps most durably—of gender. And, it hardly bears pointing out, *who* is responsible for *what*, within families, has been a hot-button issue in America for more than a generation.

Particularly interesting and important aspects of Sonia's observation, however, and the anecdote she tells, are her use of the word "nurture," which she says more than once, and more specifically its application to fathers rather than mothers: to her husband, to her son-in-law. It is a *soft* word, a *loving* word; the responsibility that it connotes is clearly different from the brass tacks economic support and hard-edged discipline that we have more traditionally thought of as a father's primary roles.

Traditional Families, Radical Choices

Ángel and Sonia Nieto, along with their children—and now their grandchildren—are a useful place to start an examination of how the image and reality of fatherhood have changed in America: When Ángel assumed the role of stay-at-home parent for his eldest daughter, Alicia, in the early 1970s and subsequently for his second daughter, Marisa, who was born in 1976 and whom the Nietos adopted when she was six months old, he wasn't on the cusp of a wave of change—as, it might be argued, his son-in-law is now. Rather, he was on the wave's leading edge. Now in retirement, taking care of his granddaughter Jazmyne, he is going around again.

How he got to be a stay-at-home father in the 1970s provides some insight into the pressures—and the opportunities—that are bringing an increasing number of men into the domestic sphere[1] and making visible the men who have been there for some time without attracting much positive notice.

In some ways, the fact that the Nietos were willing to break new ground, willing to structure their lives unconventionally, makes perfect sense; they are politically progressive people who started their married life during a period when both discussion of and working toward revolutionary change were acceptable norms rather than aberrations.

In many American households in the 1960s and 1970s, women discovered feminist writers, and the ideas unleashed created domestic havoc. In the Nieto household, it was Ángel who gave Sonia the early, radical feminist anthology *Sisterhood Is Powerful*, because he thought she would find the essays it contained interesting and useful.

Ángel Nieto is a tall man, over six feet. In his early sixties when we met, he had gray hair, tousled, thinning only slightly; he was unshaven. He spoke softly and slowly, his English heavily accented, his affect a mix of courtly and casual.

"Politically," he recalls, "we were interested in the change of roles. My wife was reading feminist books by Betty Friedan and people like that. And I was buying those books for her."

He ascribes part of their motivation for his staying home to care for their first daughter to those influences. But finances were also a factor.

"I was working at the Spanish tourist office [in New York City]," he tells me, "and then she got pregnant. And we thought that someone should stay home with the kid. She stayed for three months and then taught as a substitute teacher one day a week for three months. When Alicia was ten months old, I quit my job and stayed home while Sonia went back to work. She was making more money than I was."

Sonia has spent most of her career on the cutting edge of the bilingual and multicultural education movements; the fifth edition of her widely used textbook *Affirming Diversity: The Sociopolitical Context of Multicultural Education* came out in the spring of 2007. When she gave birth to Alicia, she was teaching at P.S. 25, the Bilingual School, in the Bronx.

The Nietos subsequently moved to the Pioneer Valley, in western Massachusetts. Between 1975 and 1979, Sonia worked on her doctorate in education at the University of Massachusetts (UMass, Amherst). On receiving her degree, she worked for the Massachusetts Department of Education for a year and then joined the faculty at UMass as an assistant professor. The economic logic of having Ángel stay home with their children remained compelling as Sonia's career advanced. Working around the children's schedules, he took part-time assignments teaching Spanish at some of the local colleges. In 1985, he began teaching bilingual social studies and Spanish full-time at a local public school, in nearby Holyoke, the job from which he is now retired.

He felt supported within his community, among his friends, he said, as a stay-at-home father. In the 1970s, as now, that particular area of western Massachusetts, with a critical mass of colleges and universities and a countercultural feel to it, was a more accepting environment than most for a broader range of family configurations.

Ángel describes a comfortable fluidity in how work was divided in the household, to some degree how it is still divided. If you saw that something needed to be cleaned, he says, you cleaned it; if there were dishes in the sink, you washed them. As to finances, "there was money on the table," he says, and they didn't fight over that either.

"I used to do most of the work," he says, "because I was home, but she used to cook most of the time. Now I do all of the cooking."

He describes a similar division of roles with respect to their daughter Alicia.

"I used to play more with her, with the blocks, for instance, making castles and things like that. My wife used to talk to her more. She'd talk to her in English and I'd talk to her in Spanish, so she grew up bilingual."

Practical details aside, he emphasizes that they had strong philosophical motivations as well.

"We have a commitment to social justice," he says, "to antiracism, to volunteerism. So we try to live our lives according to our principles."

While a variety of characteristics make them logical people to be on the cutting edge of social change, in some ways the path Ángel and Sonia ended up taking is surprising; both grew up in essentially traditional environments.

Ángel was born in Cuenca, Spain, about a hundred miles southeast of Madrid, in 1940 and grew up in a mostly conservative environment, in the aftermath of the Spanish Civil War. The right-wing dictator Francisco Franco took power the year before Ángel was born, and Franco was still in power more than twenty-five years later, in the mid-1960s, when Ángel left for the United States.

He and Sonia met in Madrid, where she was working on a master's degree in Spanish and Hispanic literature from the New York University Graduate Program in Spain.

Asked about the division of labor in his childhood home, Ángel says, "There was no division of labor. My mother did everything."

His father worked outside the home; his mother was responsible for the cooking, the cleaning, and the children, though she had some domestic help from a *señora,* a housekeeper. Ángel helped out as well. The question of who did what wasn't something that was argued over or even really discussed. He professes not to have thought much about these issues then or—either as a child or as a young man—about how he would want his own family life structured in the future.

One of five siblings, he had three younger brothers and an older sister. His interactions with them, and the way their lives have turned out, suggest a few noteworthy strands beneath the surface of a childhood fairly conventional for its time and place.

In adulthood, two of his brothers came out as gay.

His sister suffered from an enlarged heart, which made exertion difficult for her. The family lived in a second-floor apartment and, from the time he was a teenager, it was Ángel who would carry her up the stairs when she came home from any excursion. Her condition was serious and ultimately untreatable. She died at age twenty-one, when Ángel was nineteen.

Sonia's parents were born in Puerto Rico. She was born in Brooklyn and grew up in the Williamsburg section of the borough, with a sister who was a year older and a brother who was three years younger and autistic. For twenty years, her father worked in a Jewish deli on Delancey Street, on Manhattan's Lower East Side. Then he bought a bodega in Williamsburg, eventually selling it and buying another one a few blocks away on Myrtle Avenue. He worked sixteen-hour days, seven days a week, taking off only every other Sunday afternoon. Sonia's mother ran the household and also worked in the family bodega, "almost every single day," Sonia says.

In many ways, Sonia's family was also very traditional.

"Not only did my mother do all the cooking and cleaning," Sonia remembers, "but when my father got home, she served him; rarely did she even sit down with him."

Her father had a small-business owner's facility with numbers—Sonia recalls him rapidly toting up figures on brown paper bags—but little more than an elementary school education. When it came to the matter of his *daughters'* education, however, he was fiercely supportive. This was no small matter in the 1940s and 1950s, when the goals most fathers had for their daughters were simply marriage and children. It was also an important support and counterweight at a time when teachers were openly disdainful of the possibility that a Latina could pursue higher education.

But Sonia points to another respect in which her father, in which her family, was different.

"My father broke some stereotypes," she says. "*He* was really the nurturer in the family more than my mother was. I think she had a very difficult childhood; it was very hard for her until much later in her life—probably in her seventies—to show a great deal of affection."

It makes sense that Sonia's childhood experiences would incline her toward a more nurturing man when she married. It makes sense that Ángel's early and intense experiences as a caregiver would imprint him with both how important and how gratifying that role could be.

Whether or how Sonia's younger brother's illness impacted her ideas about family configuration is an open question, as is whether or how the sexual orientation of Ángel's brothers affected his views. Certainly, his brothers would later impact how Ángel was seen, in relative terms, on the "scale of conventionality."

When Sonia and Ángel visited Spain with their young children, she recalls, people were surprised to see how Ángel took care of his children. In Spain in the 1970s, however, Ángel's life, no matter how far he had departed from the traditional role of the father, would surely have been seen as much more conventional than the lives of his brothers.

"When I went back to Spain with my daughters and my wife, people there were amazed," Ángel recalls. "They saw me with my daughter [in a carrier] on my back, and they couldn't believe it. For them it was shocking to see this change of roles."

The Next Generation

Alicia and Celso Lopez's house is smaller than that of Alicia's parents. Both the yard and the house itself are cluttered with kid-related plastic, the toys and the tools of modern childrearing: baby bottles and a sippy cup on the living room coffee table, a yellow Fisher-Price car with blue wheels and an orange seat parked next to the couch. When I arrive, Celso is napping with the children upstairs so Alicia and I have a little time to talk alone.

In her midthirties, she has her mother's smooth, prominent cheekbones; a similar voice, with some of the same notes in her laughter; a bit of her father's height; dark eyes; and short, dark hair to her shoulders. When Celso and the children come downstairs, still a little drowsy-eyed, Celsito looks somewhat formal, a four-year-old banker or academic on his day off, in a pinstriped blue and white Oxford cloth shirt and jeans. Celso is wearing olive corduroys and a red and white checked shirt, his dark hair fairly short, an unruly cowlick— sleep-related or not—near the back of his head and just off to one side; he's slightly heavyset and unshaven. The baby is in pink socks, a pacifier on a ribbon pinned to the shoulder of her striped onesie. Clarita, not yet two, has on magenta pants with flowers on them and a pink top; her hair is in two short pigtails, which look a little like tufted sprays of grass, at disparate angles on either side of her head.

Like his father-in-law, Celso Lopez is from Spain. He was born in Cádiz, on the southwest coast, the oldest of five brothers. His father was a naval officer. When Celso was in his teens, his mother opened a flamenco academy, one of the first women in the area to work outside the home, to start her own business. Although his education was mostly business oriented, he has largely worked as a teacher in the United States. When we met, he was staying home with his two daughters full-time and Celsito was in day care. Alicia was teaching middle school Spanish in Amherst.

When Celsito was born, they were living in New York City. Alicia was teaching at a private school on Manhattan's Upper East Side, and Celso did not yet have the papers he needed to work in the United States. Alicia taught virtually right up until she gave birth, took six weeks off, and then went back to work, closely paralleling what her parents did when she was born. In part, she says, the question of who stayed home with the baby at first was a functional matter. But then she also had the model of her own childhood; she had no doubt that a man could be a good stay-at-home parent.

Alicia describes herself as broadly satisfied with the division of child care that she and Celso have worked out. He's home with the girls during the day. When they're both home, they trade off in most of what they do, and they have some loose guidelines: Sometimes one of them cooks dinner, sometimes the other; whoever makes dinner is responsible from beginning to end, from setting the table to cleaning up the kitchen; sometimes he takes care of bath and bed time, sometimes she does; bath and bed go together too. And when one of them can't quite manage cooking *and* cleaning up, or bed *and* bath, they adjust; theory and practice don't always match up perfectly.

Around the edges, Alicia sometimes finds herself frustrated. There is essentially no child-care task that her husband will not take on, she says, but he often needs to be prompted.

That's a common issue in households where shared parenting is practiced. We might think of this as emotional or administrative labor. That is to say, even when men are doing fully half the physical labor of child care (or more)—bath time, bed time, feeding, diapering, dressing—often, it is argued, a woman is in the background, *directing* these activities, giving the prompts:

"Have you changed her yet?"

"Is he hungry?"

"Won't she be cold that way?"

This sort of less visible labor may mean that women reap less respite than they might from this sharing of duties.

What fathers do or do not do, with what degree of competence and with what level of initiative or enthusiasm, is a matter of some debate. And the terms of that debate are often sharp. You can find and fling around numbers to support any position you want to take about who's doing how much and the direction in which change is going: hours of outside-the-home work going up or down, changes in the relative amount of time men and women spend caring for home and children. But the core of the issue is emotional, not statistical.

Women complain—with justification—that how mothers take care of their children is the subject of a great deal of ongoing societal scrutiny and criticism; men don't get off easy here either, however. In her book *The Cultural Contradictions of Motherhood*, for example, Sharon Hays argues that a father's participation in child care sometimes creates more work for the mother, not less.

"Whatever the reasons," she writes, "mothers 'know' that most men are simply less attentive to the needs of children than women are. And this means that asking a male partner to take more responsibility not only feels a bit like beating one's head against a wall but also that, even if the wall should give a little, it still *behaves* like a wall when it goes about the task."[2] Researchers, commentators, and critics have regularly described the way in which some men go about performing domestic labor as a matter of conscious strategy, essentially sabotage: Throw one red sock in with the whites and your "incompetence" has exempted you from ever doing laundry again. But from another angle, part of what we are seeing today is a kind of territorial tussle over who rules the domestic turf—the flip side, perhaps, of the war that women and their egalitarian male allies have had to fight to get anything approaching parity in the professional sphere.

At home or at work, change doesn't come without . . . change.

"I've had to let go of some things," Alicia says, about how the house is run. If she wasn't the one performing a task around the house or taking care of the children, perhaps it didn't have to be done to her standards. Even if she *was* the one doing the task, she laughs, perhaps standards needed to be reexamined.

That seems right.

After all, keeping a five-person household running is a radically different proposition from keeping a two-person household running. And it would be hard to argue, to my mind anyway, that the kids would be better off with her spending time putting all the toys away (just so they could take them out again) than with her spending time reading to them.

These changes, this ongoing negotiation of how the house should run, have clearly not been easy for her. But the benefits are clear as well: She's raising her children *with* her husband, not *for* him; there is no question about her professional or financial competence, her ability to succeed independently. Moreover, this struggle to adapt is not one-sided. She also recognizes that Celso has made tremendous adjustments too. He grew up in a house with a maid, she says; he almost never had to make his own bed, prepare his own food, wash his own dishes. Women served men. He saw that in how his father was treated as well.

And yet—*Celso has become Ángel.*

How? Why?

Celso's response provides an interesting counterpoint to both Sonia and Alicia.

"You do what you have to do" is his primary answer, repeated several times.

As to his childhood, he says he and his brothers *did* have to make their beds, clear the table, help around the house in a variety of ways.

And one of the sources he cites for this pragmatism is somewhat counterintuitive: his father, the naval officer.

"He's doing this stuff that I don't think his father would ever have dreamed of doing," Sonia said of her son-in-law.

Celso disagrees. His father did *everything*, he says, including work around the house, cooking, cleaning. He certainly didn't do those things anywhere near as often as his wife did—and Celso laughingly recalls that he did not always do them well—but he did them.

In significant part, he puts this down to his father's serving in the military. Yes, the military is a fundamentally conservative institution, and it was so particularly under the Franco regime. But military organizations are also pragmatic: Everything needs to function; people need to eat; quarters and gear need to be kept clean. In the end, the imperative is to get things done; it matters less *how* they get done or who does them.

At the time we spoke, Celso was wrestling with problems that afflict most stay-at-home parents: Some days with his kids were longer than others; sometimes he had a little cabin fever. But he said he was comfortable out and about with his daughters, taking them to the park, taking them with him to the store.

He was also somewhat concerned about family finances and thinking about finding at least a supplementary job. The classic problem, of course, was that if he were to work outside the home, just as a starting point, he would have to be paid enough to cover day care for three children—no small hurdle.

The work/finance issue was just as pragmatic as the question of who took care of the children. He didn't feel that there were any identity issues involved with being a stay-at-home father. As to the imperative to work outside the home, regardless of gender, this was also not an issue, he said.

"We Spanish don't have the Protestant work ethic," he said, with a laugh.

Interestingly, Celso and Alicia agreed that he was more likely to spend time playing with the children than she was, and thus they were more likely to go to him to play games and to go to their mother for more practical needs.

The same had been true of her father when she was growing up, Alicia pointed out.

What Is a *Machinchar*?

The Nietos are thoughtful, articulate people. Talking to Alicia, to Ángel and Sonia, to their son-in-law Celso, gives some insight into how they've structured their lives and why, what they believe, how they feel. But because Ángel is a writer, as well as a teacher, there are other angles from which their family history can be viewed and from which Ángel's role as a father can be examined.

Anthropologist Clifford Geertz has famously written, "Culture is the set of stories we tell ourselves about ourselves."[3] In so doing, one thing we do is create a record of who we are—or who we think we are. But writing does not merely reflect reality; we also use it to construct, or to reconstruct, reality—to describe who we would *like* to be.

While taking care of his daughters, Ángel kept a kind of diary for each: his observations about them as they grew, bits of their artwork, stories he made up for them, poetry he wrote about them. Alicia has the memory book her father wrote for her; Ángel showed me the book he wrote for her younger sister, Marisa.

This is private art, personal communication. But there is a more public record as well.

In 1993, Scholastic brought out a short children's book that Ángel had written, with illustrations by Stephanie O'Shaugnessy, called *El Machinchar: Diálogo en Dos Voces*. Written in lyrical, rhyming Spanish, it tells the story of an unnamed father and his daughter, Alicia.

The father has style problems; he doesn't much care how he looks, and he doesn't have much of a sense of what goes with what. When he walks down the street—he tells us and an illustration shows us—people stare in amazement as he passes by; even infants and animals are aghast. Early on, he gives a rueful, self-deprecating description of the daily quandary of clothing selection:

> Los colores mezclaba
> de una forma muy rara
> y por mucho que trataba,
> casi nunca acertaba
> y la ropa combinaba
> de forma desatinada[4]

> [The colors would mix
> very strangely
> and as hard as I tried
> I almost never got it right
> and the clothes would combine
> all crazily]

The daughter is his ally in trying to work out this problem. And—perhaps because she has not yet reached her teen years—her attitude toward her father, though sometimes exasperated, is never mocking. She wants to help; he knows that he needs her help. So, morning after morning, he asks what goes with what. And morning after morning, she tells him about combination after combination, "No, not that. That doesn't go [*que eso no pega*]."[5] Finally, the daughter tires of this daily routine and decides to resolve the problem. She says to her father:

> con cariño y sin malicia
> —Papá, eres una calamidad
> debes aprender a coordinar.
> Te voy a hacer un "matching chart"
> y verás cómo así lo lograrás[6]
>
> [tenderly and malice-free
> "Papa, you're a calamity
> You must learn to coordinate.
> I'll make you a 'matching chart'
> And you'll see how it'll work out"]

And, of course, with his "matching chart" (*that's* what a *machinchar* is, the transliterated Spanglish part of the book's title) tacked to the inside of his closet door, the father lives stylishly ever after. The final scene of the book shows him confidently striding through the neighborhood, looking "*bien arreglado, elegante y coordinado*"[7] [well put together, elegant, and coordinated], everyone who sees him looking on in admiration. The last stanza tells us that this is a true story; the last line, also in Spanish, is "Alicia is my daughter, and I am her father." The biographical note at the end of the book tells us that a number of the poems and stories that the author has written for children are based on experiences he had as a stay-at-home parent.

El Machinchar is an interesting book on a number of levels: in the attitudes that it bespeaks toward language, ethnicity, authority, family, and—most interesting to me—gender roles. First and foremost, it is completely centered on the relationship between the father and the daughter. Indeed, no other family members are represented at all: no mention, no evidence in the illustrations. We can project anything we want onto the blank spaces left on the canvas: The father may be a single parent—for any number of reasons; he could be gay; or there could be a wife and/or mother, someplace "off screen." What we are shown in the story may be some part of a nuclear family; it may be a nuclear family in its entirety.

It works.

The two clearly love each other. Their mutual respect is such that Alicia helps her father rather than mocking him, and the father is willing to accept, and be guided by, the sartorial authority of a child who appears to be eight or nine years old. While the book is written almost entirely in Spanish, the daughter's use of the phrase "matching chart" suggests a household in which at least two languages are in play, in which "code switching" is so unremarkable as not to deserve or require any overt mention or explanation.

The power of the story is that it does what writing teachers of all stripes often exhort their students to do: It *shows* more than it tells; it is in no way preachy or didactic; it sketches a warm domestic landscape without footnotes, explanation, or apologies. It is highly effective in making a number of points, in significant part because it doesn't read like a book that is "trying to make a point."

Humor helps here as well; the mood of the story is light. There is also a deft layering of roles, traditional representations interleaved with a series of inversions. The father is the primary, the *only*, parent we are shown, a somewhat unorthodox role. That his fashion problems require female intervention is familiar ground in terms of gender representations. That the solution to the story's central problem is a child facilitating an adult's success in "learning how to dress himself" tacks back in the other direction again.

Shifting Family Structures: Who Benefits?

It is noteworthy that this true story from Alicia's childhood in the 1970s didn't make it into print until the 1990s. While the Nietos' domestic arrangements were surely not unique in the 1970s—rare, certainly, but not unique—encouraging the visibility of men in those roles was not a mainstream concern until relatively recently. The image of a man doing that kind of work, acting in that particular role has long been too odd to be considered "salable." Then, as now, there was far more attention focused on "working mothers" than on "stay-at-home fathers." Only in the past few years have stay-at-home fathers—or the more numerous "equally sharing fathers"—hit the cultural radar screen in sufficient numbers to make such families an identifiable, and potentially profitable, market segment. Mix René Descartes' "I think; therefore, I am" with Adam Smith's observations about the power of the market and we get: *We buy; therefore, we are.*

It should be stressed here that this is in no way a "men versus women" plaint, an argument about who deserves more sympathy or attention. As a statistical matter, women working outside the home still vastly outnumber men who take responsibility for children and domestic labor, in whatever degree. No argument. But a greater focus on men in nontraditional roles would inevitably benefit *women* more than it would any other group.

The feminist promise of the 1970s notwithstanding, *none of us* can "have it all." There are still only twenty-four hours in a day, seven days in a week. If you do "this," you can't do "that"; we can go without sleep for only so long. The flexibility of our domestic situations—or the *lack* of flexibility—creates fundamental limits on the flexibility of our work situations. "Freeing" women to work outside the home isn't liberation if they still remain responsible for the great bulk of housework and child care. Rather, it results in what some have dubbed "the double yoke."

How do we avoid this problem?

A contradiction and a not very deeply buried ambivalence exist that we have to face up to first.

In the 1960s and 1970s, when women's fight to gain entry to and equity in the workplace really took off, one could argue that a good deal of what they were fighting for was power; they were fighting to get in. That was a difficult fight; it isn't over yet. But the goal made political, intellectual, and—perhaps most important—emotional sense. Women had been locked out of a variety of "boys' clubs," kept at financial and professional disadvantage.

Battering down the doors was the right thing to do.

Consider the situation in the domestic sphere, by way of contrast. Women who felt that they had been locked in the kitchen or in the nursery could batter down those doors from the inside and come out into the sunshine of a broader range of options; many did.

But doing that didn't necessarily pull men into those spaces to pick up the slack.

On the right, it has been argued for some time that we've experienced a kind of domestic vacuum as a result: "No one's home," they say.

On the left, men have often been criticized for "not pulling their weight at home."

Let me be perfectly clear: From my point of view, the "correct" domestic arrangement, the best way to take care of home and children, is what each couple or each individual family agrees on between/among themselves. If that means both partners work outside the home and split the domestic work, fine. If it means one partner stays home and takes primary responsibility, fine. If people looking in from the outside don't think the arrangement is reasonable or equitable, too bad.

How we run our families is personal business—political business, yes, but still personal.

Let me also be perfectly clear that I *don't* believe that the primary reason men do less at home is that women are resistant to giving up authority over the domestic sphere. If I had to give a one-word reason, I would cite inertia. Change is never easy.

I *do* believe that this resistance is a real factor, however, that part of what is going on in many homes today is a conflict over territory, over domestic turf. Women may know, intellectually, that giving up some of their power in the domestic sphere is necessary if men are to do more of that work. Emotionally, however, I believe there is an understandable ambivalence.

Fighting to gain power feels better than giving it up.

The conflicts that Alicia and Celso Lopez have had over who does what at home and over *how* things get done—to whose standard—should be viewed through the lens of this ambivalence. I would argue that they have been successful in sharing the domestic work in significant part because they have been able to face and to process this issue directly and because Alicia has recognized that for Celso to move toward doing this work, she has had to move back a bit. Things are not being done exactly as she would do them, but they are getting done.

In *El Machinchar,* the father gives up some authority over how he dresses, ceding it to his child. In return, because she has a keener sense of style, he reaps a public benefit; people on the street respect and admire him more. Similarly, in real life, some measure of Sonia Nieto's success is the result not merely of Ángel's moving into the role of taking care of home and children—and thus freeing up more time and energy for her to devote to her professional life—but of her making the space for that to happen. A similar dynamic is at play in her daughter Alicia's marriage.

On the occasion of *Ms. Magazine*'s twenty-fifth anniversary, in the fall of 1997, Gloria Steinem wrote, "[W]omen will never be completely equal in the workplace until men are completely equal in the home."[8]

She was right.

Sometimes, to get something, it's necessary to give something up.

2

The Problem of Language: Can Fathers *Mother*?

I saw an actual father!
But there was something wrong with something he did
He and his son were climbing up in a tree
And somebody said that he'd kidnapped the kid

Well then the mothers they all started screaming
And pointing at the man in the tree
The sharpshooters arrived and they shot the man dead
You know that that guy, he could've been me!

—LOUDON WAINWRIGHT III,
"Me and All the Other Mothers" (© 1988 Snowden Music)

It's not easy being a mother, is it?" the librarian says, smiling over my shoulder, as I change my six-month-old daughter's diaper on a desk in the back room.

I close my eyes very briefly, try not to grit my teeth, remember to breathe.

"I'm not *being* a mother," I tell her, as softly as I can manage. "I'm *being* a *parent*."

"You're doing what mothers usually *do*," she tells me.

And I think it best to let the conversation die there.

I don't have the time, the energy, or the tact to respond.

Situations like that were almost a daily occurrence when I was out and around with my daughter when she was an infant, and often it was as if I'd lost my voice; I am by nature a combative person, but if parenthood does nothing else it tests the limits of your energy and endurance.

Even your outrage has to be carefully rationed.

On that particular day, I had been "invited" to work, to score entrance exams for the freshman writing course that I was teaching; I was taking care of Rebecca four days per week that term, but, in a fit of the kind of flexibility that I realize is rarely extended to working mothers, my department chair had simply suggested that I bring the baby with me for the morning rather than miss all the fun.

So I came in early, folding playpen in tow, took my daughter into the back offices in the library, where we were going to be working, stripped her, fed her, cleaned her up, changed her, and got her dressed again, while the librarians buzzed in and out, doing their work.

But there's always commentary.

Does it sound lighthearted, a slightly cynical, but essentially harmless, observation about statistical reality—perhaps even well meant, an honor accorded an *exceptional* man?

Does complaining about this make me seem thin skinned?

Try this if you're a woman who works outside the home, particularly in one of the professions, a doctor, a lawyer: Someone observes you at work and says, "It's not easy being a man, is it?"

Lighthearted? Well meant? Essentially harmless?

In today's atmosphere, a statement like that is closer to legally actionable.

What irritated me about what the librarian said didn't have to do with law or even etiquette, although both of those lurked in the background—was she creating a hostile work environment for me? Rather it hinged on issues of language.[1]

The Second Half of the Language Revolution

First-wave feminists were quick to point out that the language we use has a profound impact on how we see ourselves and each other, how we interpret the world and our roles in it, what we see as possible and what we lack the words even to describe effectively.

How has gender-related language changed in the last thirty years or so?

I would argue that we've had an incomplete, one-sided, linguistic revolution: We've done a great deal to truly neuter the neuter pronouns and other terms that, in English, have traditionally been male.

We've seen this most clearly in the professional sphere, in how we name different jobs. And we can glimpse something of a loop there, a cycle in which women break into different aspects of the working world, the language begins to change as a result, and that change in language opens up the possibility of more women entering that space.

To be clear, women were not kept off police forces into the latter half of the twentieth century, for example, because grammar kept them out, but both little girls and little boys might logically feel either invited into or warned away from a variety of job possibilities depending on how we name them.

I saw this myself when my daughter was four years old.

Could she be a fire*man* when she grew up? I asked her.

No.

Could she be a fire*woman*?

Yes.

What about a fire*fighter*?

That sounded too violent to her.

"I don't think I'd want to *fight* the fire," she told me, "I'd just sit and watch it."

And there you have the Law of Unintended Consequences, up close and personal.

We wanted to use gender-neutral language to increase her sense of her own possibilities. She heard the word "fighter" as violent.

Call her a literalist or call her a politically correct toddler; sometimes when we try to solve what we see as old problems, we end up creating new problems:

Fire*pacifier*, anyone?

Or does that sound too much like a hypoallergenic, latex-free nipple, soaked in chili sauce?

The degree to which we have processed or accepted these newer gender-neutral words and usages varies by age, region, and political orientation. But the institutional battle is essentially over, even if implementation can be uneven: College writing programs routinely require nonsexist usage, as do the style books of all the major publishing houses; when you call a department head a "chair" rather than "chairman," people scold you that you've referred to that person as a piece of furniture with roughly the same frequency that people are told that "a *kid* is a young goat—not a child!"

All of the examples so far have been about language changes in the professional sphere, however.

What about the other side, the language of domestic work, the words we use to describe the roles usually ascribed to women? Change there has been decidedly slower: It is still the case that while "to mother" conjures images of caring and nurturing, "to father" essentially means to inseminate. The somewhat antiseptic phrase "to parent" may be gaining ground as a verb—and warming up—but reflexively, as with my librarian friend, what people fall back on when referring to caring for children is woman-centered language.

This matters.

Looking at the words "father," "mother," "parent," "family," and "home," looking at how we have applied them in the context of child care in the last thirty years or so, tells us a lot about where we've been and where we may be going, about what has changed and what hasn't changed.

Writing more than twenty years ago, in *Language and Woman's Place*, Robin Lakoff observed that to call a man a "professional" identifies him as a doctor or a lawyer or someone else in a respected occupation; to call a woman the same term implies that she is a prostitute. Similarly, to be a "master" is to have power over something or someone; to be a "mistress" is to have an illicit sexual relationship. She identified this "lack of linguistic equivalence"[2] as one of the keystones of inequality.

She was right. And it cuts both ways.

Some opposition to linguistic change has been straightforwardly presented as a bulwark against "the barbarians at the gate," the alternately dangerous or frivolous notion of gender equality.

Some opposition—sometimes sincere, sometimes disingenuous—has been represented as a "pure" concern for aesthetics or grammatical continuity. Often, the argument is made that language "as it is" is neutral and that attempts to change it represent an inappropriate intrusion of politics into vocabulary, grammar, or usage.

In *Man Made Language*, Dale Spender sets out the rationale for the impact of gendered language on how we construct social reality and thus both present and future possibilities. In particular, she takes issue with the idea that the construction of language is values-neutral, free of ideology or intention:

> Names are human products, the outcome of partial human vision and there is not a one-to-one correspondence between the names we possess and the material world they are designed to represent. We are dependent on names but we are mistaken if we do not appreciate that they are imperfect and often misleading: one of the reasons that people are not led to the same view of the universe by the same physical evidence is that their vision is shaped by the different names they employ to classify that physical evidence.
>
> Naming, however, is not a neutral or random process. It is an application of principles already in use, an extension of existing "rules."[3]

She's right too.

What pushes or impedes changes both in how we live our lives and in how we describe them?

Any number of factors, but I'll focus here mostly on four:

1. **Egalitarianism:** The ideas about equality and justice that America's "designers" got from the Natural Rights philosophers and wrote into our founding documents, as in "All men [*sic*] are created equal."

In his "I Have a Dream" speech, Martin Luther King, Jr., referred to that phrase as a check, albeit one that had bounced.

Of course, "All" is not exactly what they meant: It didn't mean African Americans; it didn't mean Native Americans; it didn't mean the landless, or indentured servants; and it certainly didn't mean women.

King's response was "[W]e refuse to believe that the bank of justice is bankrupt."[4]

And our history has been a herky-jerky process, a slow and uneven progress, toward making "All" *really* mean "All."

2. **Tradition:** We may resist change out of political conservatism, a belief that it is necessary and right for things to remain as they are; we may also resist change for apolitical reasons, simply because change can be disorienting, may make us feel torn loose from the moorings of "how things have been."

3. **Economics:** Whatever we believe, however we may *want* to organize our lives, economic factors can create incentives and disincentives either for change or for stasis.

   In the context of family and child care, the rise in the last thirty years or so of the two-earner household has clearly played a significant role.

4. **Self-interest:** Finally, what we do and how we talk about it are impacted by what we think is best for "us," whether we use that pronoun to cover individuals, families, a miscellany of subcultures that we either identify with or reject, or society as a whole.

"Home" and "Family"

While the verb "to mother" is more closely associated with nurture and the verb "to father" remains more associated with *begetting*, the past quarter century has seen these words begin to flex.

"Mothering" has been used, at least sometimes, as a gender-neutral term, to refer to fathers taking care of children; increasingly "fathering" has been expanding to encompass nurturance as well as simple paternity.[5]

It is, however, in the usage of "home" and "family" that we have seen the greatest changes. Home is a place; family is a group; both contain more room than the unitary images of "mother" or "father." In the shifting of meanings and uses of the words "home" and "family," we can trace a kind of *constructive destabilization* (I realize that a more conservative analyst would see, and name, this rather differently) one result of which has been increasingly meaningful inclusion of men in domestic work in general and child care in specific—and increasingly open recognition of this trend.

One core element of the resistance to change in the words "mother" and "father" has been the intertwined question of religion, spirituality, and identity—most of these essentially arguments about tradition: What does it *mean* to be a father? What does it *mean* to be a mother? To what degree are these roles flexible, and to what degree are they preordained either by biology or by theology?

There has been similarly heated and emotional debate about the words "home" and "family."

"Family Values" has been a buzzword and a powerful battle cry for some time now. In the argument over "home" and "family," however, there is a counterweight, a range of deeply pragmatic and functionalist forces working in favor of change.

Some of this opposition comes from the ranks of feminists and other egalitarians. Impetus has also come from economic pressure to redistribute domestic labor, as the two-earner household has become the norm. But movement in this area has also been abetted by a web of additional constituencies and concerns—gay families, adoptive families, interracial families, among many others.

A condensed version of this argument would be that American society in the past twenty-five years has begun to acknowledge a broader definition of what "family" means, and language has both facilitated and followed that change. If our previous definitions of family have had more to do with blood and with law, we are now increasingly willing to allow this definition to be more a matter of function and of choice: In this model, we become families by living together and/or caring for each other, by actions that we take, rather than via biology or external sanction; we become families by choice.

This can be tagged as part of an egalitarian impulse: *Why should your definition of family be considered more legitimate than mine?* But there is a libertarian cast to this argument as well, one of those moments when the political spectrum arcs, rather than simply running in a straight line, when left and right bow around and meet out back.

You can see this sentiment succinctly expressed in a bumper sticker with the diversity rainbow that reads, "Hate Is Not a Family Value," a clear rhetorical move to expand "family values" across the political spectrum rather than making it only a slogan of the right, a rebuke to conservatives who reject the very idea of gay or single-parent families.

On the utilitarian side, concern for order and efficiency—for economic benefit—is also pushing change. It is *useful* for people to be cared for by people who love them—and who don't have to be paid.

In cases where people's lives have become entwined but no mechanism officially recognizes this, any number of matters that are clearly defined for a married couple can wreak havoc: property settlement and custody questions after a relationship breaks up; survivor or pension benefits and questions of medical power of attorney in cases of death, illness, or disability.

These issues are most obvious in the case of same-sex couples. But they apply as well to aging friends who choose to live together, children informally taken in, people with disabilities who may live "independently" but together.

A strong economic incentive exists for society to support and to normalize a broader range of families. The same imperatives are pushing us to broaden what we mean by the word "home."

The deinstitutionalization movement that began in the middle of the past century has made the word "home" much more prevalent, and more broadly used, than it had been in the past. It has also had a significant impact on the meaning of the word: In many ways, the *word* has been deinstitutionalized, as well.

When first used in English, in the mid-nineteenth century, according to the *Oxford English Dictionary* (*OED*), to refer to places like "The Home for Confirmed Invalids," the meaning was explicitly institutional.[6] The neighborhood-based, scattered site "group home," however, the bane of every NIMBY (Not in My Back Yard!) movement, has made great strides since the middle of the twentieth century, as the more usual repository for people who had previously been kept in larger, more impersonal, more isolated institutions. These homes are meant to more closely mimic family homes.

The mentally or physically impaired, the elderly, troubled teens, recovering addicts, parolees being eased back into society, battered children or adults seeking shelter from abusive relationships—all of these groups have fed demand for "group homes."

And while we are constantly told that not enough of these homes exist to fulfill myriad needs, their numbers are growing; with them spreads a broader usage of the word "home" and, to a lesser degree, the word "family," a kind of rhetoric of family and support being one of the keys, therapeutic and otherwise, that make these facilities more "human scale" and more effective in helping a broad variety of people.

In the categories of "family" and "home," we find an odd and interesting coalition of political points of view that have a stake in supporting change: Progressives see the creation of therapeutic or supportive communities based on a family model as an alternative to large, inhumane institutions; economic conservatives see this as "local control" and "decentralization"; social conservatives revere "family values" as an almost universal solution to society's problems.

In the area of adoption, meanwhile, a venerable tradition long underpinned by law, both liberals and conservatives have increasing reason to *out* what was, for most of the twentieth century, a quiet practice:

Post–*Roe vs. Wade*, antiabortion campaigners have a stake in strengthening and legitimating adoption as an alternative to abortion. This has aided and abetted people supporting a variety of interracial, cross-cultural, or international—and therefore inherently more *visible*—adoptions.

As a society, we do not necessarily agree on what the roles of mothers and fathers should be, on who should take care of what—and that ambivalence is evident in our language. We have little to quibble about, however, in the idea that "family members should take care of each other" and that "home should be a functional and supportive place."

Tamar Lewin outlined the utilitarian case for this position in a November 4, 2000, *New York Times* article entitled "Is Social Stability Subverted if You Answer 'I Don't'? Fears for Children's Well-Being Complicate a Debate over Marriage," writing in part:

> Martha Fineman, for example, a professor at Cornell Law School, would end marriage as a legal category, and turn the nation's attention, instead, to finding broader ways to support those who care for children, the elderly and the disabled. . . . "I would like to see all the social subsidies redirected toward caretaking. For children, the important thing is that there be enough adults to care for them, whether it's by married biological parents or two or three or four others. If that's what we want people to do, that's what we should focus on, not marriage." (p. B-11)

How you respond to Fineman's argument depends a great deal on your beliefs and your personal situation. Some Americans may see proposals like this as attacks on marriage and on the family as it has traditionally been defined. For others, expanding what we mean by home and family is simply a matter of allowing our language (and the law) to catch up with the reality of how we live our lives.

"Fathers," "Mothers," and "Parents"

The definitions of "mother" and "father," in both noun and verb forms, from the *OED* give us a fast list of basic meanings. Logically enough, both parents are associated with creation and with care, but as a matter of *order,* the male parent is earlier and more often identified with creation and the female parent with care.

As a noun, the first definition for "father" is given as:

1. a. One by whom a child is or has been begotten,[7] a male parent, the nearest male ancestor. Rarely applied to animals.[8]

It is not until the fourth definition that we get a description that includes nurturance—and even then it is mixed in with a number of words that imply a kind of "tough love." A father's care comes in the form of protection, and with a variety of debts attached, chief among them a debt of obedience:

4. a. One who exercises protecting care like that of a father; one who shows paternal kindness; one to whom filial reverence and obedience are due. (In OE [old English]. applied to a feudal superior.)[9]

This comes directly after a definition that is decidedly weighted in a more cool and calculating direction:

3. a. One who institutes, originates, calls into being; a constructor, contriver, designer, framer, originator. Also one who gives the first conspicuous or influential example of (an immaterial thing). *The Fathers* (U.S.): the framers of the constitution. [10]

"Mother" as a noun shares a similar first definition:

I. 1. a. A female parent; a woman who has given birth to a child. Correlative with *son* or *daughter*.[11]

But in this case, the issue of nurturance comes up much more quickly, in the second definition offered, and while care is also defined as a kind of protection, a mother, rather than being due obedience, is due affectionate reverence:

2. *fig.* Applied to things more or less personified, with reference either to a metaphorical giving birth, to the protecting care exercised by a mother, or to the affectionate reverence due

to a mother. a. Said of a quality, condition, event, etc., that gives rise to some other.[12]

The verb forms show a parallel similarity in the first definition and a corresponding asymmetry in how high up on the list the question of nurturance is raised.

For "father" we are given

1. *trans.* To be or become the father of; to beget.[13]
3. To act as a father to, look after; to carry out (a law).[14]

For "mother" we are given

1. *trans.* To be the mother of, give birth to; in quotes. *fig.*, to be the source of, give rise to, produce.[15]
   2. a. To take care of or protect as a mother.[16]

It is worth pointing out, in the contrasting definitions above, that to "mother" includes both care and protection. To "father" includes "looking after," which has a more passive sense to it, as well as a legal meaning unconnected to parenthood.

In day-to-day usage, men taking care of children *do* get called mothers. This can be said with warmth and with good humor, or it can be said with varying degrees of derision. Whatever the intention, this runs up—hard—against gender definitions that are often less flexible in the real world than they are in publishing house style books.

In the song "Me and All the Other Mothers," for example, folk singer Loudon Wainwright III ruefully details the ongoing experience of being the only male on the playground with his child and points to some of this dissonance:

> Yeah, we're sippin' on our coffee containers
> Chit-chattin' tellin' little white lies
> Labor-horror-stories and painless abortions
> I wasn't feelin' like one of the guys[17]

You can read the word "guys" in that stanza in at least two ways, both of them revealing.

He could be using "guys" to mean "men," in which case being a dad on the playground makes him feel less of a man; he could be using "guys" as a gender-neutral word, referring to the group of mothers on the playground, a group he can't really be part of; he could mean both.

There has been something of an expansion in the primary meaning of and a "warming" of the word "father" as a verb form. Some women and men with egalitarian motivations use "to father" as the equivalent of "to mother." Some men do this as a matter of self-interest, because they feel it more accurately reflects their experiences.

In print, this usage was first evident in texts produced for a progressive audience—in *Ms. Magazine* and *The Nation*, for example—which would have been better cued to immediately understand the change. But more recently there has been some seepage into more mainstream contexts.

In January 2005, for example, in the *New York Times Sunday Book Review* section, Helen Schulman's review of Nancy Rawles's novel *My Jim*—which tells the story of the slave Jim, in Mark Twain's *Huckleberry Finn*, from the point of view of Jim's wife—included these lines:

> [Jim's] compassion and selflessness gave Huck the only loving parent he'd ever known. That Jim had been agonizingly torn from his own children only seemed to increase his hunger to *father* this castaway.[18] (emphasis added)

At the nexus of politics and public health, there is also a growing movement that emphasizes "responsible fathering," such as the For Fathering Project mentioned earlier.

Characterizing fathers' groups is difficult, however. They range from pro-feminist egalitarian groups like Dads & Daughters, which focuses in part on fathers helping their daughters develop and maintain positive images of themselves—a counterweight to destructive popular culture images of women and girls—to much more conservative groups that essentially argue that the maintenance of marriage and male prerogatives is the key to healthy families and stable society.

In 2001, referring to this latter tendency, Eleanor Smeal, president of the Feminist Majority Foundation, argued, "There's this whole myth that's created by the [fatherhood] movement that it's [i.e., poverty and social problems are] the woman's fault. From the very beginning, feminists wanted to share child rearing, diapering, taking kids on picnics, to the park. This is not about that. This is about saying 'I'm going to be the social engineer by coupling up women with men, whether they want to be or not.' "[19]

I am not arguing that the Fatherhood Movement represents utopian progress, but it's not simply malign retrogression either. This is an extraordinarily diverse group that doesn't agree about much: from the neopagan followers of Iron John to the Born Again Christians of the Promisekeepers; from the organo-groovy ponytailed fathers, with their kids in Snuglis to angry divorced men fighting child custody laws and their ex-wives—and not necessarily in that order; from private, public, and religious social welfare agencies focused on teen fathers in poor urban communities to grassroots movements that have sprung from those same streets.

Smeal is certainly correct that for *some* of those men and *some* of those groups, male responsibility for children means a return to traditional patriarchal control of both the children and the household. For others, however, responsibility has an egalitarian cast to it with which she would surely agree.

These changes aside, the *OED*'s itemizing "to look after," as detailed above, as one of three possibilities in the third definition of "to father" lingers. And that definition is particularly apt with regard to popular perception, which often has it that women *actively* "take care of" children, while men—at best—*passively* "look after them," one implication being a propensity to watch them do destructive or dangerous things without intervening.

In *Thinking about the Baby: Gender and Transitions into Parenthood*, Susan Walzer's study of new parents, Walzer uses the word "fathering" to mean "taking care of," rather than simply "begetting," a child. Nevertheless the discussion around this usage often *heightens* the difference between "fathering" and "mothering" rather than normalizing it and setting it up as an equivalent term, as in this passage, where her interviewees discuss "the good mother" versus "the good father":

> In contrast to the lofty expectations for mothers, Ken said that what society expects of fathers is "being a provider for the family and just . . . not abusing your family in any way." Mandy argued that people are more suspicious of fathers, and perceive them as disciplinarians who "need their time away and . . . are not always there" for their children: "And that's really a bad stereotype because most fathers out there I think just love their children to death. They just love them." Yet Mandy didn't think that society equated love with fathering.[20]

In addition to changes in—a greater flexibility of—the verb "to father," there have been at least some attempts to make the verb "to mother" more inclusive.

Diane Ehrensaft, for example, author of *Parenting Together: Men and Women Sharing the Care of Their Children*, tells readers early on, "My major interest in this book is in parents who 'mother' together because they *choose* to and not because they *have* to."

Tied to the asterisk is a note at the bottom of the page: "'Mothering' is used here to refer to the social and psychological acts that are done by the primary caretaker, regardless of the gender of the person doing them."[21]

Fathers reading that sentence might experience a bit of ambivalence: appreciation for the act of inclusion; irritation on one level or another that being included as a parent seems to mean changing gender.

Hybrid terms—"Mr. Mom," for example—have enjoyed some success as well.

Mr. Mom is not necessarily a good role model, however; it is the title of a movie (1983) in which the father loses his job and is *forced* to stay home and take care of the kids because his wife is better able to make money.

This loss in status is humiliating, and his performance, as caretaker for both his children and his house, is comically inept. Although some men have proudly taken on this title, for most the gender-bending aspect of the phrase is awkward at best, if not downright insulting.

The country song "Mr. Mom" by Lonestar (2004) follows essentially the same arc as the movie: The song's narrator loses his job; his wife says she'll go to work to fill the gap; being "Mr. Mom" sounds cool to him: TV and naps.

But of course that fantasy quickly disintegrates in the face of the difficulties of child care and housework—and the fact that a man is just not up to the task—ending on a sweet but ambiguous note: He used to think that what she did was easy; now he knows better and acknowledges this.[22]

Does that appreciation translate into a different division of labor or fleeing the strain of kids and cleaning as fast as possible (back to the sanctuary of the workplace)? Only Mrs. Lonestar knows for sure.

One possible reason for the marginally greater success in changing "father" rather than "mother" is that *expanding* "father" involves gain: Men gain from a more accurate description of what they do as fathers; women benefit from that expansion as well.

Opening up the word "mother," however, involves loss: Women have to "share" the title; men get a title that doesn't quite fit. Again there is the matter of territory.

One source of resistance to changing these words is that "mother" and "father" have long had deep religious and spiritual significance to a broad range of people, who remain both overtly, and sometimes subconsciously, averse to having these meanings tinkered with.

We can see this in Christian tradition in the phrase "Mother Mary."

The phrase "Mother Earth," meanwhile, brings together a broad coalition from difference feminists to ecologists to a wide swath of people whose spiritual beliefs and practices center on the idea of a more embracing and balanced goddess—an alternative to the historically male deity of the three major western religions, dubbed by some, Gore Vidal among them, the Angry Sky-God.[23]

That women should resist "sharing" the word "mother" makes sense; it is one of the most powerful terms they "own."

In Chapter 6, I examine the movie *Kramer vs. Kramer*. In one of the climactic courtroom battle scenes, where divorced parents played by Dustin Hoffman and Meryl Streep spar over custody of their son, the use of the word "mother" as a weapon is striking.

"I don't know how anybody could believe," Streep's character says at one point, "that I have less of a stake in *mothering* that little boy than Mr. Kramer does" (emphasis added).

This puts the argument on a linguistic plane that fatally disadvantages her ex-husband, who has been taking care of their son since she abandoned the two of them.

His response recognizes and attempts to correct this.

"I'd like to know," he asks the court rhetorically, "what law is it that says a woman is a better *parent*, simply by virtue of her sex?" (emphasis indicated by inflection in the movie). The "mother" card, however, trumps the "parent" card—in the movie, and, for most of the twentieth century, in law—rather decisively.

One of the problems with "parent" as the natural gender-neutral alternative to either "father" or "mother" is that it is less specific.

"Show the reader," we urge students in writing classes. "Make us *see* what you are talking about. Be *specific*."

We can talk about child care with a cold, utilitarian practicality, paring down our definition of caregivers to functional roles, as in the article by Lewin mentioned above.

It is difficult to quarrel with a statement like "Offspring require care to maximize their survival potential." And we can extend this to address the larger society: "Poorly cared-for offspring result in reduced efficiency and survivability of the larger social group."

Neither of these, however, has the warmth, the power, or the concision of "Children need mothers."

Nevertheless, "parent" has made some genuine progress, as both a noun and a verb. Of thirteen examples of this usage given in the *OED*, for example, the majority (seven) come from the 1970s, with an additional three from the 1950s. In other words, we are using the word in newer ways; we are changing and expanding its meaning.

While we may view this use of "parent" as progress, one might question how much warmth or nurturance it conveys.

Imagine seeing a child with a scraped knee crying on the playground. What impression is conveyed by saying that the child *needs mothering* versus saying the child *needs parenting*?

To me, the former conveys warmth, the latter a rather more neutral, almost "supervisory," kind of attention.

But this may be changing: "To parent" and "to father" may be warming up; "to mother" may be opening up. All of that would be good news for children everywhere, with knees either scraped or unscathed.

We need to take care of our children; we can agree on that, I think.

The Language of Parenting: What Are We Saying? How Much Have We Changed?

It makes sense that the impulse toward tradition, toward keeping things the same, toward resisting change is particularly strong when it comes to language.

Language is the most important early learning experience for us as children, the skill that opens most of the educational and experiential doors that follow. We strive, for years, as our power over language increases, to "get it right," both to internalize and to be able to appropriately voice the attitudes and ways of seeing the world required by our time, our place, our culture, our subculture.

We are constantly corrected in these attempts, by parents, by peers, by teachers; it makes sense that, after this constant, early, and forceful imprinting, we should have some discomfort with fundamental change.

As a writer and as a teacher of writing, I see this professionally all the time. The language of high school and college students being the most fluid—the engine of slang—I find myself, year after year, a little farther away from the way my students communicate. And I am forced to make ongoing decisions and adjustments in what I deem acceptable or unacceptable in my students' work.

Language has been an important part of the evolution of the professional sphere, an active area of battle, in which people have fought for, and won, a measure of change. Some of this has been in the service of *recognizing reality*: the reality that women have always done more than society has acknowledged, linguistically and otherwise; the reality that women have been moving into new areas in increasing numbers. Some of this has been in the service of *facilitating change*, of creating a linguistic landscape in which children grow up—and into—an environment that allows them to be whatever they want to be.

In the end, it is likely that the language of the domestic sphere will succumb to the same changes that have affected the professional sphere, both facilitating and mirroring change: The presence of female police*men* lent weight to the movement to use the phrase police *officer*; the revival of that usage made it easier for girls to picture themselves growing up to do that job.

In the same way, the "seepage" of men into domestic roles will likely spur language usage that will both acknowledge and validate contemporary domestic reality and create linguistic windows that enable boys to picture—and to *name*—a future for themselves in which they too are permitted, even encouraged, to nurture.

All of these changes taken together, this opening up of what "family" means, benefit men who choose to be more active and nurturing caretakers of their children. In the context of the—decidedly mythical—1950s suburban American housing development, populated exclusively with middle-class, white, Protestant nuclear families made up of a working father, a stay-at-home mother, 2.3 of their biological children, and the requisite pet, a stay-at-home father stands out as a radical deviation from the norm.

Let's put this same father into the same development and populate it a little more realistically: on one side of his house we might find a gay couple with an adopted daughter; on the other an Indian immigrant, his Jewish wife, and their three children; down the street there's a divorced mother raising her son; across from her house is a group home where six kids with multiple sclerosis live, along with two house parents and a rotating support staff.

In that landscape, the stay-at-home father is suddenly closer to the 1950s Ur-Father played by Robert Young on *Father Knows Best*. In a sense, then, in both linguistic and practical terms, men who take on more active parenting roles are riding the coattails of feminist activists but also of a broad coalition of people with a stake in opening up the definition of family and of family roles.

Almost eight years after my experience in the back room of the college library, I was at a school picnic and helped a child with some spilled ketchup. The commentary that I got in that instance was from another parent—a stay-at-home dad named Tom Andrejev. And Tom's use of language said a lot about how the role of "fathering" has changed and how it continues to change.

The story of his family is the subject of Chapter 3.

3

. . . .

Tom Andrejev: The Matter of Trust

. . . .

I believe in putting the resources in up front. That's
going to send your child off on the right trajectory.
I liken it to a space shot. If you're half an inch off on
earth, you're a hundred thousand miles off by the
time you get to the moon. That's how I see it for my
children.

—TOM ANDREJEV

'm at a picnic at my daughter's school, waiting on line to get lemonade refills, and a kid a few feet away from me misses his hamburger and unceremoniously squirts ketchup on the front of his shirt. I snatch a wad of napkins off the table that holds the lemonade coolers and hand them to him.

Next to me in line, Tom Andrejev[1] says, "A father is always there."

I don't know the kid, I don't know the parents, and Tom doesn't just mean that fathers are there for *their* children.

He means if you're a father, you take responsibility for children almost generically; if there's a child near you in need of help, you provide the help.

I like Tom's attitude, but I like his language even more.

A number of years earlier, at a holiday party at the local Jewish Community Center, where my daughter was in day care, I had quickly leaned in and righted a three-year-old's cup of punch, just before it spilled. And one of the women standing nearby had smiled in approval and said, "Just like a mother," intending, more or less, to say something complimentary but still managing to raise my blood pressure a few points.

Tom is on the thin side and long limbed. He wears wire-rimmed glasses and often has his brown hair cut in the same style as that of his youngest child, his son, Anthony. His elder daughter, Clea, was twelve years old when I spoke to her recently; his younger daughter, Elizabeth, is a year younger than my daughter; the children were born at roughly two-year intervals, in 1994, 1996, and 1998.

Tom's first postcollege career was as a marketing executive in the rail freight industry. Then he took twelve years off to stay home and take care of his children full-time. In the summer of 2006, feeling that they were old enough for him to go back to work, Tom took another job in the industry, in a rather different area: as a freight train conductor, riding the rails and working the yards instead of riding a desk. Little more than a year later, he went back to being a stay-at-home dad.

Tom's wife, Rachel, is a physician. She has brown eyes and black hair, generally pinned up and elegant when she goes to work, frequently down on her shoulders when she's at home. She wears wire-rimmed glasses as well. She's somewhat petite—at twelve, Clea has just caught up with her in height.

Tom and Rachel met in 1985 on a flight between Baltimore and Newark. Rachel was then pursuing a master's degree in public health; Tom was working for a rail freight company in Baltimore. He quit that job in 1987 and took a job with ConRail when the two of them moved to Philadelphia together, so that Rachel could attend medical school. They married the following year. Rachel became pregnant in the last year of her medical residency, took four months of maternity leave after Clea's birth, and then went back to work.[2] Tom quit his job in August 1994, to stay home with Clea full-time.

Twenty years after Ángel Nieto became a stay-at-home father, one would think it would be substantially easier for a man choosing this path. That hasn't been Tom's experience.

Somebody Needs to Stay Home with the Kids

Both Tom and Rachel were the youngest in families with four children. He grew up in Leicester, in Central Massachusetts. She grew up in New York City, in Queens, a nine-and-a-half-year gap between her and her closest sibling, which sometimes made her feel more like an only child. Into early adulthood, the idea of having her own family wasn't terribly appealing to her.

"As a younger person," she says, "I would have said that the state of the world was in such upheaval that I wouldn't want to bring other people into the world, to inherit it."

As to the division of domestic labor in her family when she was growing up, the boundaries between who did what, Rachel says, were traditional, and "they were set in stone."

Tom cites facets of his childhood that convinced him early on that, when he had his own family, it would be important that his children have a stay-at-home parent for the first five or six years of their lives.

First of all, he says he was raised by two very loving parents, albeit in a household with a thoroughly traditional division of domestic labor.

Rachel concurs with Tom's description of his parents, particularly his mother.

"I think that his mother *embodies* maternal love," she says. "I don't know how else to put it."

Second, the fact that Tom's mother was home with the children when he was growing up was a keystone to his childhood. He felt taken care of and taken seriously. He enjoyed being with his family, being with the kids in his neighborhood. He wanted a similar experience for his own children. From a very young age, he was offended by the "children should be seen and not heard" ethos that adults in the 1960s often espoused, many of his aunts and uncles among them.

Finally, when Tom was in his midteens, his older brother—then nineteen or twenty—started his own family. Ultimately, he would have three children, and Tom became an early and an active uncle.

These factors led him to the conclusion that it was important that *someone* be at home with small children—he was less concerned with the question of who, and I'll get back to that; a conviction that children are to be treated as people, that they are to be respected; and the realization at a relatively young age that he was comfortable being with, that he enjoyed being with, young children.

His ideas about home, about family, and about gender roles were also shaped by the fact that he had two older sisters. Although the division of labor between his parents was traditional and bright-line clear—his father went to work, mowed the lawn, worked on the cars; his mother did cooking, cleaning, and child care—what went on between the children, and between the children and their mother, was a bit more fluid. He did the dishes with his sisters; his mother always made it clear that "we share the burdens together."

During one of our conversations, Tom and I were at a campground on Cape Cod, talking while Anthony—then six and a half—more or less orbited the picnic table where we sat. Tom's priorities, his values, what he wanted to inculcate and encourage in his children, were clear from the way he talked to Anthony, as was the link back to what Tom's mother had taught him by example. Love and responsibility were the dominant themes.

"You are a person who can really love," he said to Anthony at one point. "You take good care of your stuffies [stuffed animals]; you take good care of our animals at home; you take good care of your friends at school, both older and younger, and your classmates. I see that and that's a good thing."

If the loving mother—or the loving parent—is something between truism and cliché, Tom's mother also provided a model in a number of other ways, strength of conviction at the top of the list.

Principle was important to her.

Justice was important to her.

And these were not merely abstract notions; she believed that there were times when it was important to fight for these values.

Leicester is in Central Massachusetts, in northern Worcester County, in a region that was the cradle of the industrial revolution in the United States but has, since the mid-twentieth century, become better known for what used to be manufactured there than for what is still manufactured there.

Tom's father worked in the steel industry. Summers, when he was in college, Tom worked for the Norton Company, a multinational conglomerate that still produces abrasive products, from grinding wheels to sandpaper.[3] And up through his childhood, the national shoe manufacturer and retailer Thom McAn had a major production facility in nearby Worcester, the county seat and New England's second largest city.

In family lore, Tom's mother's tussle with Thom McAn is emblematic of how she taught her children to fight for principle—and a demonstration of the fact that such fights could be won.

She received a notice in the mail in the late 1960s of the "Come on down and claim your prize" variety. It appeared that the family had won a Florida vacation. But, of course, when she got to the shoe store there was no vacation on offer, just the "opportunity" to buy shoes.

She was incensed.

Her time had been wasted.

She had been misled.

She didn't stop at letting the people in the store know that she felt this was wrong. She went to the company's top management, and she kept going after them until she got satisfaction.

The family never did get that elusive and illusory Florida vacation. But when the smoke finally cleared, the company had apologized to her for the misrepresentation—and, in compensation, provided a free pair of shoes for each member of the family.

If his childhood experiences and the example of his mother were important to Tom as models of what he wanted for his own children, it's worth asking why this didn't lead him to attempt to re-create that situation in his own marriage. Why didn't he seek simply to marry a woman who would run the kind of household that his mother had run?

Part of Tom's response is functional, focused in particular on their joint financial needs at the time they started a family; part of it is emotional, focused on what he needed, on what Rachel needed, and on what they came to agree their children would need, on what they wanted them to have.

"[When Rachel was] in medical school and residency, I was earning the income," he says. "I was the sole income provider to support the two of us and everything that we did. Right at the end of her residency, when we started a family, simple economics dictated to me that, in the context of what I wanted for my children, it would have to be Rachel that would be the income earner."

As a physician, she had the greater earning potential.

And, as Tom describes it, for two lower-middle-class kids with a heavy debt load from their education, every dollar counted.

"I didn't have the freedom to stay home at that point in my indebtedness" is the way Rachel puts it.

While Tom was the one who had the initial and stronger concern about someone staying home with their children, this was a feeling that Rachel came to share.

"At some point I thought about becoming pregnant while I was in residency," she says, "and Tom had a very strong feeling that one of us had to stay home."

Initially, she adds, "I didn't say the same thing. But when I actually became pregnant, I was happy that he had chosen to stay home."

Manning the Home Front

Anthony and Elizabeth and Clea have grown up so far with their father at home, as primary parent, and seeing their parents switch off as necessary in caring for them. But certain rhythms have been fairly consistent, with the dominant theme being time, and timing: They know that it is almost always their father who gets them up and ready and out in the morning, almost always their mother who puts them to bed at night.

Medical problems that come up before, during, or after school are dealt with by Tom, evening and weekend medical problems by Rachel—though, as a physician, when the problems are serious, she can obviously bring to bear a greater measure of expertise whatever the time or the day of the week.

Rachel does the shopping and the cooking in addition to working full-time; Tom mows the lawn, takes the garbage to the dump, does home maintenance; they both do laundry and house cleaning—as well as hiring some outside help in that area. Tom is "on" with the kids weekdays during working hours. Rachel picks up most of the evenings and weekends; they haven't done much in terms of hiring outside child-care providers.

Rachel says it often feels like they are constantly trading off.

She comes through the door from work, and it's *Tag, you're it!*

They flex when they have to. The kids know, for example, that part of Rachel's work is an almost constant round of studying: for a variety of medical licenses and renewals, to keep up with the literature. For a brief period, she worked for an insurance company in nearby New Hampshire, which sometimes necessitated her staying there overnight once or twice a week: planned absences. And sometimes, during the winter, it entailed getting snowed in overnight: unplanned absences.

Territory and control don't seem to have been major issues for Rachel.

"When I left," she says, "[Tom] was really in control of the day. . . . He got to set more of the rules because I wasn't there."

Breast-feeding was just about the only area in which she describes her role as primary.

"But he had to deal with the frozen breast milk all that time," she adds.

From the first, they essentially agreed about the larger aspects of how they wanted to take care of their children, although they didn't always agree about every detail.

"He has a much different style than I do," Rachel says. "He's very scheduled; he's very organized. I'm looser about those kinds of things. . . . My style of keeping the kitchen is not as meticulous as his," she says—the opposite of the stereotypical complaint—as well as "my style of scheduling the play dates." The transition "was hard on the weekends, when I was home and the primary parent would sort of switch. And the styles would sort of switch."

Still, she adds, "I feel fine about that. I think he's done a good job—we can't all have the same perspective on everything."

"Ultimately," she laughs, "it seems to work out. . . . The best aspect is that the children got to be a priority for the first years of their lives. It was definitely best for them."

The kids seem to agree, and this is reflected in how they think about and how they talk about what they expect their own future families to look like.

When Elizabeth thinks about having a family, she pictures her husband and her both splitting their time between taking care of two adopted children and working outside the home.

At seven, Anthony says, "I think I'm gonna take the kids to school and walk the dog—if we have one. And I think the mom is going to go shopping and go to work. I think I'm going to stay home with the kids."

When she thinks about what her own family might be like in the future, Clea takes the dividing up of domestic labor for granted; her attitude is functionalist. As the eldest of the three children, she has been more aware of her parents as a limited resource since the birth of her younger brother. With three children, two always have to share one of the parents and there's less one-on-one time. For the moment, anyway, this has led her to conclude that she wants only two children: "one per parent."

She expects to have a career.

What her husband does is more of an open question.

She expects him to have a career as well—although she had previously said that she expected him to be the at-home parent.

She expects that child care will be divided up in a way that meets the needs of the whole family.

But she also knows that plans change. At twelve years old, she can already recount a steady evolution in her thinking about career: from princess, to early childhood teacher, to obstetrician, to nurse-midwife.

Moving into adolescence, she's becoming more comfortable talking to her mother than to her father about some topics.

But at least part of this she puts down as much to style as to gender.

"She listens more and only gives her opinion when I ask," she says of her mother. "He listens, but then he gives his opinion straight out," she says of her father.

Still, asked whether or not she feels that adolescence is beginning to separate her a bit from her father, she demurs.

"We're not that separate," she says. "When I hear a lot of other people talk about their fathers, they're like, *My father was being so annoying today.* I don't really feel that way. I don't really say anything like *Oh, my dad is cooler than that* or *I have a better relationship with my dad.* That would be kind of cheesy. But . . . I don't know."

She smiles and shrugs.

"When Ya Coming Back, Tom?"

"The journey has been long and hard," Tom says, about going from being a respected professional to being an at-home-parent, from being financially well compensated and holding a position that people understood and to which they could easily relate to doing what many people still think of as *women's work*—whether they say this openly or not.

One difficulty, early but ongoing, was making clear to a broad range of people what he was doing and why he was doing it.

"Why is this guy at home with his children?" Tom asks rhetorically, the background question, often but not always unspoken, heavy in the air. "He must obviously have failed in his other world," in his professional life, he answers.

Part of what he had to do was work to integrate himself into the social networks around child care largely populated by mothers, some of whom made him welcome, some of whom were something between baffled by, resistant to, or suspicious of his presence—both around children and around them.

"There were women," he says, "who were wonderful and very supportive of me. And then—the other end of the spectrum—there were women who wouldn't give me a minute of their time and looked at me like I was a Martian."

Explaining himself to his professional friends and former colleagues was also difficult.

They could understand *some* degree of involvement with child care, but as Tom's time at home with the children stretched out, from months to years, their perplexity grew.

Where were his priorities?

That his children were his priority was difficult for them to understand. We *talk* incessantly about making our children a priority—as a society, as a community, as parents—but the brass tacks reality of actually giving up something as central as work, and the benefits that come with it, both tangible and intangible, in order to take care of children is still often looked at askance.

Professional women have complained for some time about being pulled in opposite directions over work and family, about inconsistent and mixed messages. Former Texas governor Anne Richards once said, for example, that conservatives seem to believe that middle-class families are in crisis because women are out working instead of staying home with their children and that poor families are in crisis because women are at home with their children instead of out working.

Hard to win at that particular game.

For men, there's less of a tug. Yes, we're told that we should be more involved with our kids; but very few people are encouraging—or even comfortable—in the face of a man who, for whatever period of time and for whatever reasons, actually puts children above career.

"When are you coming back?" Tom says they kept asking him. *"Are you done yet?"*

And while he and Rachel had worked out a domestic arrangement with which they were comfortable—which balanced their collective financial and professional needs with creating the kind of environment they wanted to provide for their children—even members of Tom's extended family were a little nervous about his giving up a good salary, running the risk of derailing his career.

"What are you *doing*?" Tom says they asked him on a regular basis.

Men Are Dangerous

One problem that men have to confront and ultimately to surmount when we become more involved on the domestic side, with home in general and with children in particular, is the reality that we are often seen as a threat. Obviously, this fear is not without a basis: Men commit the vast majority of murders; men commit the vast majority of violent crimes; men are disproportionately responsible for sexual assaults and molestations, including, and particularly relevant here, the physical abuse and sexual molestation of children.[4]

This reality, and the fear that it engenders, puts men in a difficult double-bind. Men are criticized, from just about every point on the political spectrum, for not being sufficiently involved in the care of our children, whether this is a conservative diatribe about men who father children and then simply walk away from any responsibility for them or the complaint—more prominent in progressive circles—that women's professional progress is impeded in significant part by the inability or unwillingness of men to shoulder their share of child care and, perhaps just as important, to open up emotionally in the ways that good and supportive parenting requires.

But what happens when we do these things, when we *are* present, when we *are* open, when we *are* involved?

We often become objects of suspicion.

Men are whipsawed between competing complaints, between *Why aren't men more involved with children?* and *Why is that guy so interested in children?*

"I saw a woman on the playground today" is, for most people, an innocuous statement; the silent follow-on is a shrug, an *of course*.

"I saw a *man* on the playground today," however, gives at least some—I would argue many—a hint of hesitation. There, the follow-on is often "What was a man up to on the playground?" and the implied answer, *No good.*

This problem is compounded by the degree to which American society has long been sex obsessed in a variety of ways. Because women still predominate in most of the social networks around children—the car pools, the day-care parent groups, the playgroups, the PTAs—a man trying to integrate himself and his children into those spaces faces suspicion not only over his motivations for wanting to be around children but also regarding his intentions toward women. That suspicion can come from the women themselves; it can also come from their husbands or partners.

Tom Andrejev has faced those problems in public; he's faced them in his children's school; he's even been confronted by them in his own home.

Five or six years earlier, Rachel recalls, "there was a cleaning woman that refused to clean our house because Tom was home, he was the adult home during the day."[5]

"We were both there when she came and looked over the house," she continues, "and she was fine and she wanted the job. Until she found out—you know, Tom said, 'By the way, I'll be the one in the house during the day'—and then she completely changed and said, 'I don't want it.'"

"He was very taken aback at the time," she adds. He began looking into lodging a complaint with one of the state's antidiscrimination agencies, "but they didn't want to have any part of it."

As an active parent at Touchstone Community School, the small private institution in Grafton, Massachusetts, that his children and my daughter attended—a visible father, a volunteer, ultimately a member of the board of directors—Tom also had to work hard to allay initial suspicion and resistance.

"In the first couple of years," Tom says, "I really had to struggle. I had to work very hard on a number of fronts to gain people's trust."

He puts some of this down to the general suspicion of men that I've already covered here. But he also acknowledges that some part of this is a by-product of fairly typical institutional hierarchy and inertia: At Touchstone, as elsewhere, you gain acceptance and move up in status by putting in your time, by being consistently present and consistently reliable, by taking on the smaller tasks, the scut work, to earn the right to take responsibility for larger projects. That holds true both for men and for women.

Tom's moving into leadership positions in the school—as chair of the marketing committee, for example, an opportunity to flex some of the professional muscles that had been dormant for a while—has something to do with a greater acceptance of men in the "active school parent" role and something to do with his cohort of parents simply moving up as the previous generation of parents graduate with their children.

That said, the matter of proving himself has never completely gone away.

"I still, to this day," he says, "have to work *very* hard—I work overtime—to demonstrate that I am motivated by goodness, that I am to be trusted, and that I have no sexual designs on anyone, male or female," child or adult.

What Did We Learn in School Today?

When my wife and I first enrolled our daughter at Touchstone, in the fall of 2000, Tom Andrejev was a notable presence on campus. He was not the only father picking up and dropping off his children, interacting with teachers, with parents, with other members of the school community. But he was, to me at least, certainly the most visible. He was also someone who acted with what might be called a higher degree of "intentionality" than most, a clear, ongoing, and consistent awareness of what he was doing, why he was doing it, and how he wanted to present himself.

At the school picnic I described at the beginning of this chapter, for example, when Tom said, "A father is always there," he was making a number of statements simultaneously and in admirably compact fashion: about how he saw me, about how he saw himself, about how he saw the role of being a father. It was not an ego-free statement, but it wasn't a long speech either; he wasn't belaboring the point. Among other things, he was making both an offer of and a request for solidarity. As to the matter of "linguistic equivalence," what he said—and the way he said it—was the perfect analogue to the kinds of statements that mothers make all the time, about themselves, about each other, and sometimes (with varying degrees of sincerity) about men.

Six years later, there were more fathers visible in the school's parking lot, dropping their children off, picking them up, chaperoning school trips. There were more fathers in evidence inside the building as well, serving as volunteers in the classrooms and for a variety of school functions and serving on the committees that keep the place running.

I have no "school census" data from the year 2000 or from any year since to back this up.[6] And when I say that I believe the atmosphere at Touchstone has become more hospitable to fathers in the same period of time, that too will have to be taken on faith, just a feeling, one person's observation.

But clearly this dovetails with Tom's experience. And I would argue that Tom's willingness to be a path breaker made it that much easier both for the men who have since become more visibly involved in the school to make that leap and for the community at large to be more accepting of this change, of this evolution.

"Any person can be what they want to be," Elizabeth Andrejev told me when she was nine years old, that commonplace of childhood—inclusive and gender neutral the way she phrased it—an expression of hope and possibility that we strive to inculcate in children at the same time that we downplay the way it might apply to adults. We are often dreamers on behalf of our children and realists—if not defeatists—when it comes to the potential for change in lives already formed and tracked, identities already ossified.

Her father has had to struggle to establish and to legitimate his identity as a full-time parent, to be what he wants to be. He has struggled with his former colleagues, with his extended family, with parenting networks, and with his children's school. He has struggled to create and to have accepted a warmer, more involved, more nurturing public profile of fatherhood.

It is ironic—and somewhat puzzling—that he has not found deeper and more consistent support for this endeavor.

On the one hand, what he has sought to do, and what he has done, can be seen as profoundly conservative: He had—and his wife came to share—a bedrock conviction that their children needed and deserved the full-time attention of a stay-at-home parent for the crucial early years of their lives.

For more than a decade, that's what he provided for them.

Erase the gender inversion, swap the parent working outside the home with the stay-at-home parent, and Tom and Rachel's family is a showcase for "traditional values."

To be sure, some conservative organizations support at-home parenting—and in Chapter 9 I look at a culturally and politically conservative family that ended up making choices remarkably similar to those of the Andrejevs.

For the most part, however, on the right, support, both individual and organizational, lines up behind *motherhood* rather than *parenthood*, behind families in which the father is the breadwinner and the head of the household and the mother is the bread baker and has primary responsibility for the children.

Interviewed on the role of Christian mothers, for example, Carla Barnhill, editor of *Christian Parenting Today,* noted, "Even though there are conservative evangelical churches that would say that the father is the spiritual head of the household, there hasn't been the same kind of pressure on a father in terms of the involvement he's supposed to have in a child's life."[7]

Specifically male-focused groups on this part of the political spectrum, such as the Christian organization Promise Keepers, urge fathers to take a more active role in the home and with their families, but they tend to espouse a rather different and rather less egalitarian view of home and family than do Tom and Rachel.

On the other hand, and at more or less the other end of the political spectrum, Tom's experience at Touchstone suggests a problematic inconsistency between what we often say in progressive communities and what we actually do but offers as well a glimmer of hope.

It has been, as Tom describes it, a tough journey, but there has clearly been progress. I see that myself, and I hear it as well in the language people use in discussing parenting issues: Active presence encourages both change and acknowledgment of change.

I stopped by the school one summer recently to pick something up in the office, for example, and ended up in brief conversation with one of the other parents, who does some volunteer administrative work there. It was a hot, sticky day, and the office was air conditioned; the rest of the building, which serves as a day camp when school isn't in session, was not.

One of her children was in camp, and she was a little concerned about the impact of the weather.

"Mother guilt," she said.

And then she amended that and said, "Well . . . *parent* guilt."

Had I grimaced, I asked—I have an ongoing problem with *irritable face syndrome*—was that why she'd changed what she said?

No, she told me, she'd simply realized, on the fly, that "parent" was the more appropriate word to use.

I would have the same concern for my daughter, wouldn't I?

Of course I would.

4

. . . .

TV Dads: One Step Forward
and Two Steps Back

. . . .

Brooke: Who would leave you with a baby?
Kevin: Why does everybody keep asking me that?

—KEVIN HILL, Episode Four, "Homework"

I spent the first few weeks of a recent school year attempting to co-ordinate one or more overlapping car pools. Quintessential parental work, to my mind: elements of scheduling and organization balanced—or thrown out of balance—by a rich broth of interpersonal issues, the fragile egos of both the parents and the children (and, of course, that of the coordinator) at the top of the list.

It was a fair fight and, in the interest of full disclosure, I'll confess that I essentially failed. My reign as Car Pool Czar was cut tragically short, and I had to unstitch those snazzy epaulettes that I had, a tad prematurely, sewn onto the shoulders of all my shirts.

It was a fair fight, though; there was no sabotage. No one tried to get me to—oh, I don't know—transport a llama, for example.

Not as lucky were the hapless fathers who appeared in the six, hour-long episodes of the short-lived NBC reality show *Meet Mr. Mom*, in which mothers were whisked off to spa vacations so that the audience could see the kind of hilarity that ensues when men are put in charge of children. They had all kinds of curves thrown at them, including the addition of a llama and a goat to an impromptu children's party.

Well, moms would all know what to do in that situation, wouldn't they?

Andean moms, perhaps.

I don't generally watch reality shows, so—personal and political prickliness aside, for the moment—what was particularly interesting to me was the remarkable degree to which these shows were scripted. How much this was accomplished via editing versus how much was accomplished because the participants, viscerally understanding their parts in the narrative arc, simply "knew their lines" by heart, is an open question. But know their lines they did.

The story in each episode is essentially the same.

A large SUV zips through streets lined with McMansions, bearing down on two unsuspecting families. Their naïveté about what is soon to befall them is odd, given that we see and hear part of this from inside the target houses, which, along with their occupants, have been unobtrusively wired for sound and video transmission.

A muscular young man delivers a scroll to whoever answers the door. The families assemble for the reading: Mom has fifteen minutes to pack and leave; Dad will be in charge of the house and the children; the two fathers must compete for the title of Mr. Mom.

Again, they all know their lines.

The mother looks smug and says, "He doesn't *know* what he's in for now."

Sometimes she cries.

The father looks a little nervous but keeps saying, "We'll be fine."

One of the kids moans, "We're doomed."

And they're off!

The families compete in a variety of tasks, usually with serious time constraints on preparation: hold a garage sale, throw a sleepover party, cook a formal dinner for guests.

But the garage sale is burdened by the presence of a cow; the llama and the goat show up for the party; and before dinner can be cooked and served, it turns out that the kitchen has been emptied not only of all food, but of plates, silverware, and cooking implements as well.

Not to worry; a madcap shopping spree at one of the show's sponsors ensues, as the clock continues to count down.

A lot of this is "I Love Lucy," more slapstick than reality, with men in the role of candy maker, as the assembly line cranks steadily out of control: chocolates everywhere—the kids will help with that!—and only so much you can stuff in your mouth at one time to try to catch up.

It's television, it's funny, and so what?

But—*now* I'll get into the prickly politics, and at this point the destination should be familiar—yes, as in other situations, it is really *mothers* who are being hurt here more than fathers. I am offended, but I'll recover.

The moral that undergirds the show is that it would be *irresponsible* for women to "let" men do more around the house, particularly with their children.

At the end of each show, the fathers say one of two things—sometimes both—to show that they've learned an important lesson: "I'm really going to *help out* more around the house" and "I don't ever want to do this again."

Put the emphasis on that last part, because that's what they *really* mean. But note as well the use of language in the first phrase:

I can "help out" around *your* house—an unexpected act of generosity—I'm not "helping" when I do things in my own house; I'm being a parent, a homeowner, a husband, a partner. In similar fashion, I can "babysit" your children, but if I'm taking care of my own daughter that's not the right word to apply.

She is my flesh, my blood, my heart; of course I take care of her.

The language tells us everything we need to know: We weren't *meeting* Mr. Mom each week; we were saying good-bye to him. The show wasn't welcoming men to the domestic sphere; it was demonstrating—yet again—that, for men, our children and our homes are alien and potentially dangerous territory.

If the women were sent on spa vacations, the men went on a kind of Domestic Wilderness Safari, into the dark heart of their own homes, suddenly sentenced to intense involvement with—*gasp!*—their own children.

Look, look, he's about to dress his son!

And he didn't even use the tranquilizer dart?

That mad, brave, fool!

Meet Mr. Mom ran six episodes and then disappeared—short summer series, canceled or on hiatus; it was hard to tell.

It wasn't a reality that I recognized, anyway.

And, frankly, I don't miss it at all.[1]

The New Man: Here He Is—and There He Goes

I do miss *Kevin Hill*, however, a prime-time "dramedy" that UPN began airing in the fall of 2004 and canceled the following spring when the network recast itself in search of a different demographic. Of course UPN itself has since been merged out of existence; its flailing about for identity wasn't frivolous; it was an ultimately unsuccessful attempt to survive.

That *Kevin Hill* didn't survive—as is sometimes the case, critics for the most part liked (but didn't *love*) the show, and it never found a large enough audience to be commercially viable—was sad and a little strange to me but instructive as well.

Jorge A. Reyes, the creator of the series, describes the show in a September 2004 article in *Newsday* as "equal parts *Sex and the City* and *L.A. Law.*"

He might have added that it also shared some crucial DNA with *The Courtship of Eddie's Father*, the 1961 Mark Toby novel, which became the 1962 Glenn Ford movie, which became an ABC TV series, starring Bill Bixby and Brandon Cruz, which ran from 1969 to 1972.

Courtship wasn't exactly a new idea when it first hit the small screen, as *TV Guide* critic Cleveland Amory noted sourly when he reviewed the show in 1969.

"For the 118th time," Amory groused, "we have a bumbling widower, a little matchmaking monster and, of course, the all-wise housekeeper."[2] I'll get to a bit more of the lineage of these shows at the end of this chapter.

The title character and the story set-up for *Kevin Hill* tweak that formula in some interesting directions: An African American lawyer living in New York City (Taye Diggs), educated, successful, stylish, and romantically busy, "inherits" the ten-month-old daughter of his closest cousin when the cousin suddenly dies. The child's mother is a drug-addicted stripper who can't be found; other family members are too old to take on an infant.

Preverbal, the child doesn't do a lot of matchmaking; the all-wise housekeeper role is filled by George Weiss (Patrick Breen), a gay nanny with a dry wit and a heavy and somewhat nasal New York accent.

"Anything else I should know about you—like drinking, smoking . . . ?" Kevin asks in the first episode, in what passes for a job interview, trying to appear thorough and professional and to gloss over his more-than-obvious desperation to get child-care coverage.

"Only in front of the baby," George replies, with a dismissive sitcom roll of his eyes.

Reyes's inspiration for the show was personal. Born in Michigan, he grew up in Buffalo, New York. His parents divorced when he was thirteen, and he and his brother Kevin—whose name was borrowed for the show—were raised by their mother, though their father, he says, "was still very much in the picture."

Reyes's cousin John had a baby with a stripper with a substance abuse problem. "She eventually abandoned him and the baby," he says, "and the change I saw him go through was part of the inspiration for the show."

He jokingly refers to his brother as an "enlightened caveman." He saw comedic potential in what might happen "if he were forced to raise our cousin's child . . . the changes he would go through."

"My cousin changed because he was a bachelor dad," Reyes says, "and his mom would not play 'surrogate mom' for the baby, so he had to leave behind his single ways . . . and it was painful for him. It took him several years before he really accepted that role fully. He still wanted to go out, chase girls, et cetera. But the family's unwillingness to let him do that forced him to grow into being the great dad he's become."

On the show, of course, things are rocky, as well: The baby immediately costs Kevin his high-end law firm job. He lands instead at a three-woman boutique law practice, headed by an African American single mother, Jessie Grey (Michael Michele), who understands his situation.

The name of the firm: Grey and Associates. Race aside—or race included, really—how Kevin's life is organized is no longer black and white.

The regular cast is rounded out by Dame (Damian) Ruiz, played by Jon Seda, another high-flying lawyer and Kevin's habitual wing man in the thin air of their upper altitude social lives, where they mostly seem to encounter actresses, models, and the occasional millionaire.

But while courtship is an ongoing and important plot thread, some of the most interesting vignettes are courtroom, rather than bedroom, dramas, focused on questions of family and of personal identity: issues of child custody, for Kevin, of course—repeatedly and at the top of the list—but also for his boss, and for parents the firm represents, including a bigamous father and a female rock star with a chaotic life.

The relationship between parents and children is also repeatedly explored in legal cases: A bereaved couple sue the school that allowed their son to be recruited into the army, sent to Iraq, and killed; outraged parents sue their son's psychiatrist; a mother sues her twenty-two-year-old daughter, who has been burning through a $7-million-plus trust fund by following bad investment advice—from her deceased father.

A number of episodes focus on sexual identity, including one that deals with a closeted gay athlete and another in which the father of a childhood friend of one of the other attorneys at the firm is denied an honor guard and burial at a veteran's cemetery because he violated the armed forces' "Don't ask, don't tell" policy. With characteristic backspin—there's the violence you expect and there's the violence you *don't* expect—George is sued for beating up a gay-basher.

Jorge Reyes has something in common with Ángel Nieto: a light touch and a sense of humor about what he is doing; the show, both in its casting and in its writing (Reyes wrote the pilot episode), regularly deals with multicultural issues, but it rarely feels preachy.

"All too often," Reyes says, "shows with people of color are defined by their need to TALK about racial issues. Life is more subtle than that. I often say we don't have to 'wave the flag' when we cast with people of color. It's not *issue-tainment*. I wanted to avoid the all-too-often-used crutch of making race the issue, just because we have a diverse cast."

"Now if a story about race comes up organically," he adds, "then fine. But I want to do stories that are first and foremost accessible. I want to show competent, complex characters and stories that happen to have people of color."

Sometimes, interestingly enough, rather than avoiding stereotyping, the show faced it head on and had a certain amount of fun with it.

In the opening beats of the fourth episode, for example, Kevin is fretting over his first court appearance to seek official, albeit temporary, custody of Sarah. He runs into the living room for fashion advice on ties from George and Dame:

Kevin: Which one says "qualified temporary guardian"?
Dame: Red.
George (*almost simultaneously*): Blue.
Kevin (*pleading*): *Fellas . . . ?*
Dame: Dude, who was voted Best Dressed, two years running in high school? Who was the youngest-ever member of Armani's legal team?
George (*cocking his head to the side*): Gay.
Kevin (*exiting*): I'm gonna go with the nanny.
Dame (*chiding George in mock exasperation*): Shame on you, perpetuating that stereotype!

What Does a Family Look Like?

Kevin's initial acceptance of custody of Sarah is tinged with issues of debt and obligation. We get a quickly sketched back-story about his relationship with the cousin who was Sarah's father: childhood buddies, just like brothers. And then the final hook: As teenagers, they were driving around one night when the police stopped their car and found a gun. His cousin took the rap and went to prison, and from there into a difficult life that ended early. Kevin went on to college, to law school, to professional and financial success: As his cousin sacrificed for him, he now feels obligated to sacrifice for his cousin's daughter. This isn't just about family—though that's no small matter—it's about the repayment of a debt.

One of the ongoing issues for *Kevin Hill*—for the title character and for the show as a whole—is how one defines family. In the opening beats of the series pilot, we hear a quick flurry of messages from Kevin's answering machine, as the camera methodically explores his elegant—and *huge*—Manhattan apartment. All of them are from women with whom Kevin has had dates, usually not many dates, usually sexually successful dates, and usually *terminal* dates: They call him afterward; it doesn't sound like he calls them back; he scores and then leaves the field, the consummate *player*.

At least one of his callers refers to him as "Daddy," but there is nothing remotely paternal about her use of the word.

Player Daddy Kevin very quickly becomes, at least intermittently and with increasing frequency, *Surrogate Daddy Kevin*, a transformation that is bewildering to him and to almost everyone around him; among other things, the early changes cost him his job—a cost of parenting we see again in Chapter 6, in the movie *Kramer vs. Kramer*: Men with children don't slowly ease into the mommy track at work; they are slammed into it.

In later episodes, the women with whom Kevin is involved either pass or fail their auditions as potential family members. Whether they like it or not—whether Kevin likes it or not—if they can't accommodate to Sarah, they can't be with Kevin: He's found a girl—ten months old—to whom he *has* to be true and whose needs, emotional and otherwise, he can't ignore.

If he neglects or rejects her, she has no one else. The impact that his inattention would have on her is immediately clear and would clearly be dire.

The cluster of fictive-family that Kevin attracts in the beginning of the series consists of his longtime friend Dame, who is the persistent voice of "let's ditch this and go party"; the members of Kevin's new firm when he changes jobs (in an early episode, when Kevin is home sick with Sarah, who is also sick, the head of the law firm stops by in the middle of the night to provide a little respite care—*that's* workplace flexibility); and, of course, George-the-nanny.

George is one of the most interesting characters; he, Kevin, and Sarah essentially form the nuclear family at the heart of the show. Kevin's response to George is measured. Kevin's a macho guy, but he's Macho Modern: too macho not to have a hint of unease with George's sexual orientation, too modern to make much of a big deal about it; the same goes for Dame. For the most part, Kevin accepts George on a functional basis, for what he does, first and foremost; for who he is, secondarily, as part of that package.

George is a competent and loving caretaker to Sarah, as well as a crisp voice of reason and reprimand for Kevin, when he needs to be reminded of his obligations.

They make a fascinating couple, platonic but tightly bound.

At the end of the same episode in which senior partner Jessie Grey shows up to bail Kevin out at home (episode seven, "House Arrest"), Kevin and George clash over how much the nanny can interfere in his employer's life.

> **Kevin:** Up until two months ago, all this I considered my island, and I was—
> **George:** The king of the island.
> **Kevin:** Yeah. Yeah. And then Sarah came along and my island got smaller and then you came along—

George: A ridiculously handsome gay nanny, and you didn't feel like the king so much any more. You're startin' to feel more like Gilligan. . . . No the metaphor's gone off track. Continue.

Kevin: Yeah, a little bit. I'm glad to have you here. And right now, you know, my life wouldn't work without you. But I need you to take care of Sarah. Not me.

George: You know when you're on an airplane and the stewardess gives the safety spiel? If the little oxygen masks come down, make sure you put yours on first, before attaching your child's? That's what I'm doing here. Taking care of you is how I take care of Sarah.

Kevin (*sheepishly*): Well it's a good thing I never get sick. . . . So, we cool?

George: Yeah. We're cool. I don't have to start calling you King Kevin, do I?

Kevin: I'm probably never gonna hear the end of this, am I?

George: Probably not.

Kevin: All right, well, you feed the kid. I'll get to work. You have a good day, man.

George: You too.

It's a credible and witty employer-employee dialogue, a tussle over "space," both personal and domestic. But—right down to something awfully close to "Have a nice day at the office, dear"—it's also not far from a spousal argument about who's supposed to do what and how things are supposed to get done, about division of labor, both physical and emotional, about boundaries and spheres of influence.

Redemption through the Child

Anyone with even a passing familiarity with women's magazines knows that the "your man as a reclamation project" article is an evergreen, a staple of the genre, spin it any which way you want:

"how to do it," "how not to do it," "why you have to," "why you shouldn't."

But the redemptive quality of contact with a child has even deeper roots, a strong Christian resonance, elements of sacrifice, of a kind of transfer of innocence: If you accept the child, if the child accepts you, then, on some level, your salvation is ensured.

Some part of this should make sense to most parents on a completely secular and functional level. Parenthood personalizes things, raises fundamental questions for us that can be difficult—or perhaps simply embarrassing—to answer:

How would I explain to my child what I just did?
Would I want my child to do that?
How would I feel if something like that were done to my child?

Part of what makes contact with a child transformative and potentially redemptive is the ripple effect. How you see the child and how you begin to see the world—through the child's eyes—changes both your relationships with other people and, often, the ways in which you *think* about relationships.

Whether your point of view is theological or therapeutic, redeeming yourself is a multistep process: You have to understand that you've done something wrong, change your behavior, accept responsibility, and—often as part of that acceptance—make amends in some personal fashion.

Kevin goes through this cycle more than once. One example comes in episode four, "Homework," the same one in which he has the fashion quandary over the color of his tie before going into court to seek temporary custody of Sarah.

He is assigned a social worker, to evaluate his fitness as a guardian, and runs into immediate trouble because he has not yet found, or taken Sarah to, a pediatrician. He lies to the social worker about this, giving her the name of a pediatrician he recently dated, and then has to scramble to the pediatrician's office, to try to get her to cover for him.

She's not exactly happy to see him.

Brooke: You're unbelievable. You fall off the face of the earth. I don't hear from you for months and then you walk in here and ask me to take a look at your *baby*? You *have* a baby?

Kevin: It's uh, it's good to see you too. I was gonna tell you.

Brooke: Right, right, but that would have entailed you actually calling me back. Who would leave *you* with a baby?

Kevin: Why does everybody keep asking me that?

Kevin's befuddlement—he literally scratches his head as he asks that last question—seems half genuine and half cover. And he spends as much energy concealing the truth from himself, with varying degrees of effectiveness, as he does concealing it from other people, not that other people are often fooled.

Later in that episode, he's in Brooke's office again—she gave in and offered an appointment for Sarah. He's late for the appointment, which is all too familiar to Brooke. She makes the comparison explicit. He's behaving just as he behaved when they dated: irresponsibly and inconsiderately.

"You know what I realized, Kevin?" she tells him, as she explains why she is sending him to another doctor, "You're a child. [Sarah's] more mature than you are."

"Well now that's just silly," Kevin responds, ever the lawyer and completely off point. "She's not even a year old."

But after a little additional dialogue, and just before the scene ends, he looks over at Sarah, embarrassed and somewhat pained.

"Don't *judge* me," he stage whispers to her, acknowledging on some level that—were she older—she would, and perhaps should. He's gone some distance in recognizing his faults, the transgressions he has to make up for, the ways in which he needs to change.

One of the key subplots in this episode is the twenty-two-year-old woman who has been losing money from her multimillion-dollar trust fund by following investment advice that a psychic channels to her from her dead father. Testifying in court, she admits that her main motivation for "maintaining contact" with her father was because she needed his forgiveness, for not having been there when he died.

When she says this, we cut to a reaction shot: Kevin's face, a moment of realization.

Being there for a child—and being there for a parent—is a lifelong commitment; what we do or fail to do in that relationship can cut deep wounds in us.

And, clearly, from the evidence right in front of him, those wounds aren't necessarily healed; that connection isn't severed, even after death.

How we address those wounds—how we either write our childhood dissatisfactions into or try to erase them from our lives as parents—and how we deal with our own parents into adulthood are central to Chapter 5, which focuses on the Smith family.

Immediately following the courtroom scene, Kevin's back in the pediatrician's office for a final visit. Initially, Brooke is surprised, and displeased, to see him, thinking he's there to pester her again. But she makes a little time for them to talk.

Kevin: I just wanted to apologize.

Brooke: Kevin, if this is about the other day—

Kevin: When we were together, I treated you badly and I'm sorry.

Brooke: Okay . . .

Kevin: You were right about everything. I had a great time with you. You were so much fun. But then we started to hang out, a lot, and it was obvious how serious we were getting and I didn't know how to put on the brakes. So I backed out. That's uh, that's what I do—that's what I *did*. Uh, I didn't want to hurt your feelings and that's why, that's why I stopped calling you.

Brooke: No kidding?

Kevin: That's it? "No kidding"?

Brooke: Kevin . . . You're *not* that complicated.

Kevin: Well, I'm working on that.

Brooke (*looking at Sarah*): So, you finally found a girl who has influence on you.

He came back to apologize, not to try to cadge medical help for Sarah. But after his apology, Brooke tells him to wait. It's near the end of the day and she can make some time to fit them in after her last patient.

Whether his redemption is complete or not—are we *ever* fully redeemed?—in part for Sarah's sake, she's willing to give him another chance, or at least not to punish the child for the sins of the "father."

Going Nuclear: Losing Sarah Grace

Kevin Hill ran twenty-two episodes, a full season, and then got canceled in the spring of 2005. The producers didn't know that the show wasn't being renewed until after they had shot the final episode of the season—although, obviously, there had been intimations. The episode would have been a cliffhanger if the show were coming back that fall; instead it became a coda. In it, Kevin loses custody of Sarah to her biological mother, now a *former* stripper and *rehabbed* drug user—albeit clean only four months—insta-married to the charismatic, smooth-talking preacher who "saved" her, in every sense of the word.

The mother, Melanie, and Pastor Gerald "Gerry" Carver—initially her fiancé, shortly thereafter her husband—appear in episode twenty-one, at the end of which they show up at Kevin's apartment, with attorney Francine Prescott (Diggs's real-life wife, Idina Menzel) in tow, to announce that they plan to fight for custody of Sarah.

The heart of the final episode, "Losing Isn't Everything," is the court battle that ensues.

Francine and Kevin "bump into each other" earlier in episode twenty-one, when Kevin attends a service at Gerry's church, during which we hear the beginning of an interesting sermon on the topic of family.

It's clear from their interaction that she and Kevin have both professional and intimate history, although we get little in the way of specifics about either. A good part of their conversation is taken up with her partially asking him about, partially teasing him about, his romantic life, whom he's been dating, how those things have been going.

When they come to Kevin's apartment, it is the minister rather than the mother who takes the lead in explaining what they are going to do and why. As from the moment of his introduction, the minister comes off a bit too smooth, his moral position and his motives both somewhat questionable, his support of Melanie tinged with more than a hint of excessive control.

While it is ironic that the minister should be painted less a figure of moral rectitude and more an object of some suspicion, that's really nothing new. Think of the evangelical huckster in Sinclair Lewis's 1927 novel—and the subsequent movie—*Elmer Gantry*. Or, even farther back, the Puritan minister Arthur Dimmesdale, in the *Scarlet Letter*, who lets Hester Prynne bear the public shame of their illegitimate child, while he takes no responsibility.

Gerry: Having had a chance to observe Sarah's environment: the alcohol, women, homosexuality—

George: Hey—

Kevin: George—take the baby away. (*To Gerry:*) What are you saying? Right now.

Gerry: I'm saying that I think Sarah should be raised in a moral and intact home.

Kevin: Like yours?

Gerry: Melanie is Sarah's biological mother and I intend to legally adopt her, something which you never got around to doing.

Kevin (*to their attorney, Francine*): So I guess running into you at the church, that was just a coincidence?

Francine: I know you're upset, but you must realize, this is for the best—

Kevin: Don't try to handle me, Francine, I know how this game is played. (*To Gerry:*) And you, you think I'm a sheep in your little flock, waiting for you to come off the pulpit and save me?

Gerry: Brother, it's not like that—

Kevin: Don't call me Brother. Don't even speak to me.

Francine: Look, if we can't handle this amicably it's going to go to court and it's going to get nasty.

Kevin: I've gotten nasty with you before, Francine. We can do it again. Now y'all get the hell out my house. Get out!

(*Ushers them out and slams the door; George reappears with Sarah in his arms.*)

George: What happens now?

Kevin: We got a fight.

George: What if you don't win?

Kevin: We're gonna win, George. No one's gonna take that little girl away from me.

It wouldn't be fair to characterize the custody battle as a fight simply over the competence of a man to raise a child. Too many other significant elements are in play: the biological mother versus a blood cousin; a single-parent household versus a married couple; a multi-pronged argument over what constitutes a "moral" environment.

But in a very real sense, the custody battle boils down to the question of who you feel has been more credibly redeemed: Kevin or Melanie.

Do we have more faith that Kevin has thrown off, thoroughly enough and permanently, the essentially masculine failings that impeded his acting as a good parent?

Do we believe that Melanie has put her sexually and pharmacologically problematic past, as well as the stain of her having abandoned her daughter not once, but twice—immediately after Sarah's birth and then when Sarah's father dies and Kevin seeks her out to sign a waiver of parental rights—far enough behind her?

Whom do we trust?

It's hard to see how we the audience could fail to come down on Kevin's side; it's his show, after all.

But it's *not* hard to see how the law—imagined or real—might come down on the mother's side. In doing so, the arguments that win *that* day—who knows what might have happened in Season Two?—are the exact negation of the case that the entire arc of the season had been making about what can constitute a stable and positive family environment.

Francine hits all of those buttons in her legal summation.

> **Francine:** While no one can take away the fact that Mr. Hill did an honorable thing by taking in a child in an emergency, if a child is to thrive, she cannot live her life in a temporary situation. And Sarah Grace should not have to, not when there is a stable home, with her biological mother, and an upstanding step-father available. Now certainly, a home with a loving cousin is better than foster care, even if the child is exposed to a nanny with an alternative lifestyle, a revolving door of strange women, and a guardian with a demanding and time-consuming career. But if there is another choice, if there is a better choice, how can we deny this child—any child—the loving, nuclear family she deserves?

Powerful words indeed: stable home, biological mother, upstanding stepfather, nuclear family. They are invoked to "save" Sarah from an emergency, a temporary situation, an alternative lifestyle, a revolving door of strange women, and a guardian with a demanding and time-consuming career; the last two accusations—intimations of promiscuity and an excessive focus on work over family—would be just as effective in criticizing a woman seeking custody.

In her summation, in Kevin's defense, Jessie Grey tries to argue for actions over titles, an argument similar to the one we will see Ted Kramer—Dustin Hoffman's character in the movie *Kramer vs. Kramer*—make in a similar situation in Chapter 6.

In both cases, titles win.

As a matter of law, we exalt "the best interests of the child." As a practical matter, motherhood, however sullied, is a tough card to beat. And the father card that Kevin has to play is symbolic rather than biological, another disadvantage for him.

> **Jessie:** Father. This isn't a role Kevin Hill sought. It was thrust upon him by the death of his cousin, and more importantly, by the abdication of her parental duties, by that woman sitting right there. However, given the awesome responsibility of fatherhood, Mr. Hill not only embraced it, he excelled. He sacrificed his place on a partner track at a prestigious firm, so that he could spend more time with his child. He hired the most qualified child-care provider he could find. And in a million other ways, put his needs second, to put Sarah's first. The Carver family, while they may appear to be nobly intentioned, are trying to remove this child from the only family she's ever known. And why? Is she being mistreated? No. Is she suffering in any way? No. So why would they suddenly appear out of nowhere and feel that this child needed to be rescued? Maybe because they're not thinking about Sarah at all. Maybe, unlike my client Mr. Hill, they're putting their needs and their desires above those of this happy, healthy toddler, who they are now trying to tear away from the most important person in her life.

"Embracing," "excelling," and "sacrificing," however, are not enough. That Sarah is "happy" and "healthy" is not enough. That Kevin is "the only family she's ever known," that he is "the most important person in her life"—neither of those points is enough either.

"Biology trumps desire," the judge says when she hands down her ruling. "Mrs. Carver is Sarah's natural mother and Mr. Hill has no legal custodial rights. I am awarding full custody to Melanie and Gerald Carver. Hearing adjourned."

If one of the important narrative threads of the show was Kevin's progress toward redemption, the character's last monologue—to Sarah, while Melanie and Gerald wait in the living room for him to surrender the child to them—tells us both that he is acutely aware of his failings and that his experience with the child has given him the ability to see himself at least intermittently with painful clarity.

He tells her, as he is letting her go, that he will always be with her, always be there for her, that, no matter what happens, he is *not* leaving her. And he gives her a rambling package of advice about how to live her life.

"You start messing with these little boys," he tells her, when he gets to the matter of dating, "you stay away from the bad ones, okay? The player types, the ones that are like me. All right? You make sure they treat you good. Okay? You knock 'em out. You knock 'em out."

Sometimes the most poignant and credible indication of how far we have come is our realization that we haven't come far enough.

The New Father: Are We Ready for Him or Not?

In the summer of 1952—in part to fill in for *I Love Lucy*, which was on seasonal hiatus—CBS premiered *My Little Margie*, arguably the first single-dad-centered TV show. The title character was supposed to be twenty-one (Gale Storm, who played Margie, was thirty-one when the series began), and she did as much to take care of her father, the widowed investment banker Vern Albright (Charles Farrell, who got his start in silent films), as he did to take care of her. She also spent as much time chasing women *away* from him—and his fortune—as she did roping them in. Still, subversive hints of independence around the edges notwithstanding (Margie had a boyfriend but he didn't seem to mean much to her, and marrying him clearly wasn't a priority), the setup was unlikely to rile traditionalists. Critics were disdainful, fans were rapt, and the series ran for three years and then enjoyed a healthy afterlife in syndication.

From 1957 to 1962, John Forsythe played Bentley Gregg, well-off Hollywood attorney and eligible man-about-town, in *Bachelor Father*. He "inherited" his thirteen-year-old niece Kelly, when her parents died in a car accident. That family was rounded out by Chinese "House Boy" Peter Tong (Sammee Tong, fifty-six when the series started), who gave sage and caustic advice and often had to be bailed out of the hare-brained financial schemes in which he was regularly ensnared—arguably the archetype of the "all-wise housekeeper" to whom Amory referred in his plaint about *The Courtship of Eddie's Father*.

Those pioneering shows were followed by, or in some cases overlapped with, any number of programs that used the single-dad motif in a broad variety of contexts: from Westerns like *The Rifleman* (1958–1963) and *Bonanza* (1959–1973); to the country-inflected *Andy Griffith Show* (1960–1968) and *The Beverly Hillbillies* (1962–1971); to more modern, "blended" families, like those on *Full House* (1987–1995) or *My Two Dads* (1987–1990).[3]

Kevin Hill shared bits and pieces of the DNA of those shows, its obvious precursors—the gay nanny being perhaps the most radical departure. It followed a time-honored formula, but it was ultimately not commercially successful.

The cancellation of a television series is a very specific kind of "failure," a decision made by a small group of people—sometimes by only *one* person—operating in a very specific context: *this* season, on *this* network that is contemplating, wooing, or imagining *this* audience. Ratings numbers—or the ratings numbers versus production costs calculation—also mean different things to different people: A show that scores fifteen national Nielsen ratings points might be a success in one context and a failure in another. A book, a CD, or a DVD release, moreover, can "wait" and allow an audience to build, hoping to profit from "the long tail." A TV series has a clearly defined and clearly limited window in which to justify its existence. It has a short *shelf life*.

I was saddened by the cancellation of *Kevin Hill*, but for the most part, I will resist the temptation to speculate on the reasons this happened or what this commercial failure might mean in broader terms.

A "comparison of narratives," however, between *Kevin Hill* and *Meet Mr. Mom* sheds some light on competing angles from which we might view contemporary American attitudes toward child care.

"Mr. Mom," as I argue in Chapter 2, is a problematic and not particularly successful hybrid appellation—how many women would want to be called "Ms. Dad"? The word, the movie, and the TV show all pivot on a view of the relative impermeability of gendered spheres of influence, certainly in the home. Outside the home, the situation is a bit different. Women can be professionals; commenting on this too much is retrograde to the point of being Neanderthal. The idea that men can be homemakers is rather more suspect; focusing on the foibles of men who move in that direction is still fair game.

We use "hitting the glass ceiling" as a metaphor for the barriers women face in climbing the corporate ladder. A good deal of the humor of shows like *Meet Mr. Mom* comes from watching men walk into the "glass walls" that mark off domestic space. You don't see them until you hit them nose first and bounce off; it's physical comedy.

We get a mixed message: Men can, men *can't*—but mostly the latter.

On the surface, *Kevin Hill* gives the same mixed message—a season of yes capped off with a legal no. But it says something rather more complicated, and ultimately more hopeful.

A Man's Just a Man, but a Family Is an Island

A pivotal moment in chapter 31 of Mark Twain's *Huckleberry Finn* is when Huck resolves that he is prepared—in fact feels more or less compelled—to go to hell.

Jim, the runaway slave with whom Huck has been rafting down the Mississippi, has been turned in for a bounty. Huck knows that the "right thing" to do is to write Miss Watson, Jim's owner, and tell her where he is. He contemplates doing this; he tries to pray; he writes the note. But then, overwhelmed by images of how he and Jim have taken care of each other on the rafting journey, he tears the note to pieces and sets off to free his comrade.

Huck does this in contemplation of two societies: the broader society, in which he knows his action is wrong and morally indefensible—in everything he has ever been taught, a violation of both man's and God's law—versus the microcosm of the raft, a society of two, in which that morality is turned upside down.

The season (and series) finale of *Kevin Hill* positions us at the same juncture, contemplating the contradiction of the larger society versus the microcosm. Rather than a raft, we have the image of an island—(King) Kevin and George have explicitly used this metaphor. The energy of the twenty-two episodes of the show has gone into demonstrating to us that the people on that island constitute a *good* family. They love each other; they look out for each other; they take care of each other.

Those tests are good enough for the writers and presumably good enough for those members of the target audience who share egalitarian and cosmopolitan values—we don't tune in to watch that family fail. How do they fly, beyond that little island, in American culture at large and on the small screen?

The argument that the Carvers make is that *they* are best qualified to provide a stable and positive family environment for Sarah. A core piece of this argument is biology—the immutable fact that Melanie is Sarah's mother. That argument is at least blunted by the uncontested evidence of Melanie's past: her working as a stripper, her drug use, her callousness in shunning Sarah shortly after giving birth and in signing her away when Sarah's father dies. The shield of motherhood is both tarnished and dented; given her past behavior, we certainly have reasonable cause at least to wonder about her future.

The other major piece of their argument consists of an attack on the home that Kevin has provided for Sarah. Gerry launches that attack when he and Melanie come to announce that they will be seeking custody of the child.

He's cut off before he can say much, but he says more than enough to be clearly understood: "Having had a chance to observe Sarah's environment: the alcohol, women, homosexuality—."

Melanie is Sarah's mother. Pastor Gerald Carver is a paragon of morality. The two of them are married. There you have the building blocks of a "proper home." Never mind that we have reason to question exactly how much to credit the first point, the truth of the second, the relevance of the third: Regardless, they are powerful banners under which to fight.

The flip side of their idealization of a narrow set of "traditional values," their secondary banner, reads: *Look where the child is now!*

She's on an island—like Huck's raft—where morality is turned upside down.

"The law is a[n] ass . . . an idiot," says Mr. Bumble, in Charles Dickens's 1838 novel, *Oliver Twist*.[4]

In choosing to save his friend, to do what he "knows is wrong," Huck Finn comes to a similar conclusion and opts for *justice* over law. It is a black and white matter, both literally and figuratively; there can be no middle ground.[5] We often speak of slavery as America's Original Sin. Huck can either redeem Jim, and thus redeem himself, or—by doing "the right thing"—damn them both.

What I see in the finale of *Kevin Hill,* by way of contrast, is a competition between redemption narratives; gender is more complicated than race. Kevin's sins have always been on full display; we've watched him commit them, and we've watched him atone. Melanie's sins were what put Sarah in Kevin's care to begin with, the animating facts, though largely offstage, that put the story in motion.

In the end, the two of them stand as "team captains" for competing families: the mother, the stepfather, and the young child versus the two men, one black and one white, one straight and one gay, one blood-related to the child, the other tied to her both by an employment relationship and by love.

I like the fact that we can argue for Kevin, George, and Sarah in that manner, as family by choice, as worthy of consideration for functionalist reasons—love being a core part of what makes their family work. I don't see this threatening or in any way diminishing the importance of traditional family structures. The question of custody is personal—it is *always* personal, in the deepest and most painful way—it is not which family structure is "better," but who would do better by *this* child in *this* situation.

I don't think the biology of gender is irrelevant here either—and I'll explore that more in Chapter 5. In the end, what we are being asked to judge is whether we find it more credible that a woman could redeem herself from a life of drugs, stripping, and child abandonment or that a man could redeem himself from failings that are largely ascribed to . . . being a man.

5

. . . .

Darryl Smith: Recovering
Our Own Fathers

. . . .

Even if parenting is hard, I don't want Sofie to feel
that she only got to know me in a short window of
time.

—DARRYL SMITH

Bob Smith died in January 2004, and I was one of a handful of white people in the black church in New Jersey where the memorial was held. His ex-wife, Josie, wasn't there; they'd divorced more than twenty-five years earlier. His brother-in-law, the Reverend Herbert Daughtry, of the House of the Lord Church in Brooklyn, preached the service. Bob's brother, Marvin, did a little drumming behind the choir and kept the heat of the crowd and the church's hardworking radiators at bay with a Japanese fan that sometimes hid his face.

I was there for Bob's son Darryl, one of my oldest friends.

We were born in the same hospital—Mount Sinai in New York City—in the same year: 1962. We grew up in the same New Jersey suburb—Englewood, a few miles from the George Washington Bridge. My parents left New York in the 1960s, in part because they wanted their children to attend good suburban public schools, and schools that were integrated. Darryl's father and uncles attended black elementary schools in Englewood before integration; his mother, Josie, was part of an interracial coalition that drove those schools out of existence.

After a fashion, that was how Darryl and I met.

I didn't really know Bob when Darryl and I were growing up. In both of our families, our parents got divorced when we were kids: He and his younger sister stayed with his mother; my younger sister and I stayed with our father.

Our parents were on the leading edge of a surge in the divorce rate in the United States,[1] and both Darryl and I, in different but perhaps complementary ways, were personally impacted by this. His experience was more typical than mine. Bob left the house in 1975, when Darryl was thirteen; statistically, that's more common. It was my mother who left, in 1978, something that is uncommon now and was downright rare then. The epidemic of divorce in the 1970s, for the most part, led to an epidemic of absent fathers.

What is the impact of an absent father?

Why is a father's influence important?

A great deal has been written and said about the social, cultural, or economic fallout of absentee dads.

A quote from Roland Warren, the president of the National Fatherhood Initiative, answers the question of emotional impact succinctly, in terms that are spiritual but also have a physical resonance to them: "There's a hole in the soul of every [fatherless] kid in the shape of their fathers."[2]

In other words, a lot of American men feel wounded, having missed crucial childhood contact with their fathers. Sometimes this has meant a lack of physical presence; sometimes it has meant a lack of emotional presence. Cut off from their own fathers, they've felt unsure, absent a model to work from, about how to connect with their own children.

Confronting parenthood, this was one of the issues that Darryl had to face.

His daughter, Sofia, is a year younger than my daughter, Rebecca. We both had tumultuous relationships with our siblings when we were growing up and knew early on that we wanted only one child. One way that both of us have tried to rewrite our own childhoods is by co-parenting our children, by making sure that—whatever we get wrong and whatever we get right—we are *there.*

But in addition to thinking about, and working on, what kind of *father* he wanted to be, Darryl also thought about what kind of *son* he wanted to be and about how he might create a healthier future by healing the past.

I believe that the actions that he has taken on both of these fronts—and, just as important, his reasons for taking them—form an important strand in the explanation of the role many American men of our generation are now playing in the lives of our children.

The Man Who Wasn't There

For me, Bob was the man who wasn't there. I saw him on rare occasions. More often, I got him as filtered through Darryl, and this was sometimes a complicated act of layering. Bob could be witty and sharp-edged; what I got was Darryl playing the character of his father, who was playing a character himself.

Darryl is just under six feet tall, muscular with a bit of softness coming on in his midforties, clean shaven, including his scalp, and wears stylishly small glasses—something he shares with his daughter. A Buddhist, he recently had a lotus tattooed onto one of his biceps.

An actor turned realtor, a community activist with political aspirations, presentation is important to him, as is style. But that's neither new nor an affectation; it's closer to wiring, really. His mother remembers him all but having tantrums as an adolescent if sharp creases weren't ironed into his jeans.

He likes knowing where things come from—the clothing he wears, the wine he drinks, the cigars he occasionally smokes—and being able to relate something of their history, to tell stories about them. He has a good voice for storytelling: deep, resonant, well modulated.

Bob was shorter than his son would grow to be, but no less stylish; his friends and family sometimes referred to him affectionately as Bob "Warehouse" Smith because of the quantity of clothing he owned. His brothers—Darryl's uncles, Buster and Marvin—were drummers who ended up playing with jazz luminaries like Archie Shepp and Sun Ra. In our teens and twenties, we'd go hear them at Sweet Basil or the Bottom Line.

Bob was a working man. He worked for a local paper company for a brief period during Darryl's childhood—shift work, which meant he saw his kids less even before the divorce. He sold insurance door-to-door for a while.

Mostly, though, Bob sold cars. As Darryl moved through high school, college, and beyond, cars, clothing, and women became common ground on which he and his father could meet, over which they could bond and relate.

While Bob loved cars almost as much as he loved clothing, he wasn't blind to what they cost their owners. Even—or perhaps *especially*—as a car salesman, he saw the humor in our coming to serve the tools that we had created to serve us. He had a collective name for the series of cars that for the most part he helped Darryl buy, starting when he was old enough to get his driver's license.

It was Bob's view of Darryl's relationship to cars that formed my strongest secondhand image of him.

Whatever car Darryl owned really owned Darryl, according to Bob, and it always had the same name: *The Big Iron Pimp*, a hulking, demanding, parasitic presence out on the driveway. Darryl would fold his arms across his chest, scowl, cock his head, look down disdainfully, and give a gravelly imitation of his father channeling the car: *I need oil! I need tires! Bring me money! Go out and sell your body for me!*

Tom Andrejev, in Chapter 3, grew up with the conviction that he wanted to provide for his children the kind of childhood that his parents had provided for him. Darryl grew up with the conviction that, in certain crucial respects, he wanted to make sure his child *didn't* have the kind of childhood he had.

Unlike many fathers in his situation, Bob didn't disappear from Darryl's life after the divorce. He continued to live in the same city, alone as a bachelor for the first few years, then back in his parents' house, where Darryl saw him regularly. They'd go to the New York

Auto Show together every year, as you might expect. They'd go to soccer games together at Giants Stadium: The newly born New York Cosmos had picked up the recently—albeit temporarily—retired Brazilian star, Pelé.

Bob also taught his son baseball. They hung out together at Darryl's grandparents' house.

But there were broad areas of Darryl's life that Bob didn't really know about: He didn't attend school events; he didn't know much about Darryl's involvement in theater or the scouting activities that filled another chunk of his time.

"He was very interested to hear about everything," Darryl says, "but he didn't go to a lot of stuff."

They really began to connect after Darryl graduated from college.

"We were close," he remembers. "We were hanging out and talking, just getting to know one another. But that was a short window."

First, Darryl moved to the West Coast.

A few years after that, Bob was diagnosed with Parkinson's disease.

For Darryl, taking care of his father—taking responsibility as a son at the same time that he took responsibility as a parent—was another important way to address unfinished emotional business. There's a spiritual puzzle piece there as well, of course. Rather than being embittered about what he felt he didn't get, he resolved both to pass forward to his child and *back* to his father some of the nurturance he didn't get.

Bob's illness was *not* what led Darryl to want him to move out to Seattle (where he and his wife lived); indeed, he had entertained the notion even before his father's retirement. But it was the illness that ultimately made up Bob's mind.

In 2001, he was living in New Jersey, in what had been his parents' house; Darryl's younger sister, Tamu, was taking care of him but also raising two children on her own, and with Bob's neurological condition getting worse, the situation became unsustainable.

Darryl and his wife bought a larger house and Bob moved in with them.

The following year, Bob had to move to an assisted living facility; he died a year later.

"What I mourn the most about not having my dad," Darryl says, "is not the dad I knew for the last five years of his life. It's the opportunity to have that deeper connection—more like I was beginning to have when I got out of college."

What he didn't get from his relationship with his father when he was growing up remains a source of some pain. His father's death, of course, still saddens him, years afterward. But he has less reason for regret than most, the comfort of knowing that he took the initiative to heal that rift, got to know—and got to care for—his father before he died, that Sofie got to know her grandfather.

For Darryl, the connection between what he felt he needed to do as a son is directly related to what he feels he has to do as a father.

"My conscious effort with Sofie," he says, "was 'I'm not going to let that happen.' Even if parenting is hard, I want to try to be an involved parent. Even if parenting is hard, I don't want that to happen for Sofie; I don't want her to feel that she only got to know me in a short window of time."

Who Does What

Darryl and his wife, Andrea, who is white, approached having a child together with a clear, shared commitment to co-parenting—rooted, to one degree or another, on both sides, in childhood experiences and convictions. Darryl grew up promising himself that he would be the antithesis of an absent father; that he would be, in all ways, *present*. Andrea grew up with a strong belief in equality, a disdainful rejection of the injustice of deciding what people could or could not do based merely on gender. They are both satisfied with the division of labor in their family—although they don't always agree on "who's doing how much of what."

But things haven't worked out quite the way they expected them to.

After graduating from Franklin and Marshall College in Lancaster, Pennsylvania—Amish country—in 1984, Darryl did theater in and around New York and Philadelphia for a few years: stage work, the odd industrial film, a brief part or two on television. Then he moved to San Francisco, to attend the graduate program at the American Conservatory Theater.

He met Andrea John in the summer of 1988. Andrea, two years younger than Darryl, had gone to school at the University of California at Berkeley. They quickly moved in together and married some two years later, making her Andrea John-Smith.

Andrea has short, glossy, dark brown hair, going salt and pepper, dark brown eyes, well-defined cheek bones with a light spray of freckles, laugh lines around her eyes and mouth, etched by mirth that is regular and often explosive. Raised in and around Los Angeles, she's an interesting mix of West Coast mellow and the sort of opinionated exuberance more often associated with the East Coast. Whatever the topic, you always know what she thinks, and she doesn't suffer fools gladly.

Almost immediately after getting married, she and Darryl moved to Los Angeles and spent a year and a half living near Venice Beach before finally settling in Seattle in the spring of 1992. In 1995, the year before their daughter was born, not bringing in what his family needed via acting work, Darryl passed the exam for his realtor's license, which put them on track toward more solid financial footing. Andrea has worked in the nonprofit sector since they moved to Seattle, first as an employee—for the Salvation Army and United Way— subsequently running her own consulting firm.

Their daughter was one of the reasons Andrea shifted her professional focus to work she could do from a home office; Darryl's work as a realtor also gives him more flexibility to set his hours around what his family needs.

"I would describe Sofie as a physical amalgam of her dad and me," Andrea says. "She has her father's round-tipped nose, café au lait skin, my fuller eyebrows, dark, almond-shaped eyes, and a round face with full pink lips. Her hair is wonderfully wild and kinky. She likes to wear it in a natural—halo-of-ringlets—style and combs it on occasion. She's tall for her age and full-figured, with a classic pubescent shape.

She looks older than she is. Her glasses are shaped like tears with tapered points at each end."

Andrea thinks the glasses make Sofie "look smart."

You don't have to listen to her much—she has the clean and mellifluous diction of her father and a good ear for language—to know that she *is* both smart and exceptionally expressive. She was nine when she talked to me about her parents, and her face was still an open book: I could watch her process questions and responses, wrinkling her eyebrows in thought on occasion, squinting as she considered her answers, her head tilting to the side now and then as she worked through what she wanted to say.

Whatever tasks are considered more fluid, everyone in the family knows that Darryl *owns* cooking. Andrea does whatever baking there is to do and fills in on an occasional basis—when Darryl is out of town, for example—but *the cook is the cook.*

He cooks with Sofie regularly, getting her comfortable in the kitchen. But, asked about her dad's cooking, Sofie suggests that his epicurean tendencies don't always mesh well with her nine-year-old palate; the language she uses to express this is deft and delicate beyond her years.

"A lot of the time," she says, "he'll make dishes that have things mixed, and things that are really different. And I don't really favor that. My mom is a more basic cook," which for Sofie is more compliment than criticism.

Sofie easily ticks off a list of who does what: Daddy does the cooking; everybody does cleaning; both parents take care of her. Darryl drops her off at school, cooks breakfast and dinner, fixes the TV set. Andrea picks her up from school, takes her to the park, does the baking. Mommy does more of the reading to her and the all-important bed-time rituals. Daddy does board games.

As to her image of her own future, it speaks to her satisfaction with the way her life is now, closely echoing what Anthony Andrejev said in Chapter 3; younger children often see their present circumstances as the template for what their own lives will be like when they grow up.

"I'm going to have it so the father will do the stuff that Daddy does now," Sofie says, "and I will do the things that Mommy does."

Her parents' negotiation of how things get done at home is ongoing. In some areas, their concerns have a useful complementarity. In cleaning the house, for example, Darryl says he's much more bothered by clutter and takes the lead in the ongoing battle to keep it under control. Andrea, he says, is more concerned about the kind of cleaning that entails scrubbing.

Of course, a good part of these negotiations is as much emotional as it is practical.

"Sometimes I do ask for more credit," Darryl says, for the things he does. But he adds, "Andrea is good about saying, 'I see what you're doing and recognize that it's important.'"

Sometimes things work by indirection.

"She'll say, '*I* really want to clean out the garage,'" Darryl says by way of example. "Meaning she really wants *me* to clean out the garage," or at least to get the process rolling.

He concedes that Andrea does more of the longer-term management of Sofie's schedule, setting up the play dates, planning ahead for vacations, and playing the lead role in some of the bedrock philosophical decisions about how they approach parenting.

They backstop and balance each other.

"If it's just the direct care," Andrea says, "I'm definitely doing more of the direct care. I'm definitely the one who arbitrates many of those primary methodologies. He's the one that says, 'You've gone too far' or 'You've missed something important.' He's observant; he's completely checked in; he's totally there."

"What he *doesn't* seem to get," she adds, "is mostly related to stuff about having to share me with her—like *get her out of our bed!* It's this whole thing of wanting to have a marriage—*dammit!*"

She laughs, and it's not clear whether the "dammit" is hers, Darryl's, or both.

She shakes her head.

"Thank God *someone's* advocating for that!"

What We Plan versus What We Do

Darryl's central motivation as a parent is fairly straightforward: He wants to make sure that he provides a consistent paternal presence for his daughter that he feels he didn't get as a child. Andrea's motivations are rather more complicated, but the relationship she had with her father when she was growing up is also central: Her father was diagnosed with cancer when she was thirteen; he died when she was nineteen.

Her father's diminishing physical presence as he fought his illness during her teen years left Andrea feeling unmoored and vulnerable into adulthood. She describes him as "the standard setter," "a role model for leadership," and—though less demonstrative than her mother—the "emotional balance point" of the family. When she talks about his illness and his death, she emphasizes not only the emotional loss but also concrete and practical losses: the guidance and the mentoring that she didn't get during a crucial period in her life.

"I wanted there to be equality," Andrea says, of her attitude while growing up—across the lines of class and race, but especially gender. "I wanted to be a women's rights advocate attorney. That's what I wanted to become."

Her mother often told Andrea that her expectations were unreasonable, that she was unlikely to be able to construct the kind of life she envisioned for herself when she had her own family.

That didn't discourage her.

"I always had a political mind, a rabble-rouser mind," she recalls. "I was always vocal about my complaints."

But the fragility and ultimate impermanence of any relationship were imprinted on her, early and deep, by the death of her father, planting the seeds of contradictory impulses.

On the one hand, she believes in an egalitarian ethic in which capabilities and possibilities are not tied to gender—or indeed to any other labels or characteristics. On the other hand, she believes that you *always* have to be prepared to go it alone. No matter the task or situation, however you plan things, whatever support you expect, you *always* have to allow for the possibility that you may have to carry on independent of outside help. The physical fact of pregnancy means, therefore, that a woman can *never* fully escape the possibility that if she has a child, she may end up the sole parent of that child.

I quoted Geertz earlier about "the stories we tell ourselves about ourselves." He meant the collective "we." Andrea might appropriate, recast, and personalize his statement somewhat along these lines: "Personality is the story I tell myself about myself."

Both for others and for herself, she sees internal narrative as key to how we live our lives, what we feel, the decisions we make. She often sees the *writing* of these stories, moreover, as physical, sees our bodies as the texts we always carry with us, our histories not merely recorded in our minds but etched in our flesh, our bones, our nervous systems, our souls.

When she talks about terror, for example—at the loss of her father, or in contemplating all the things that could go wrong with her own child—she talks about it not merely as a strong emotion but as a physical presence in her body.

I've already noted, more than once, that territoriality is one factor in how much mothers are *willing* to step back and create space for fathers to be more active parents. Andrea's example points up the degree to which some women would argue that they are simply not *able* to step back.

Some women and men would characterize this as a biological fact, a matter of brain anatomy, of evolution, of hormones, a matter of the wiring of gender—and Andrea's position on that, which I will get to, is not quite what she thought it would be when she was younger.

In this case, however, the issue is as much one of *personal* history as anything else—of personal *story*, of lessons and reflexes that she feels were embedded in her body by experience rather than by design: Andrea was just as committed as Darryl to making sure their child never felt abandoned.

Her experience as a parent also embodies the familiar tension that women have been dealing with for some time—and that more and more men are now facing—between career and family. There too, things have not worked out as she first thought they would.

In fact, talking about the period of time after Sofie's birth, when she was at home full time, Andrea says that her intention had always been to go back to work sooner. "I never, in my mind, imagined being a stay-at-home mother," she says emphatically. "Never, ever, ever. The kid I got changed my plans. The kid I got didn't sleep. The kid I got was really unhappy and physically uncomfortable a lot. And I just changed everything that I thought I was going to do."

The physical "facts on the ground" played a role in shaping—or reshaping—Andrea's career path, which took a number of turns she didn't expect. Physiology also played a significant role in shaping how the division of child care worked out in her family.

Although I've characterized Darryl as a co-parent, he isn't quite what some have called an equally sharing parent; neither he nor Andrea thinks their division of labor around child care is really even. They agree that she does more: He puts the split at about 60/40; she thinks it's closer to 70/30. Given Andrea's commitment to equality and to equity, it's a bit surprising that she evinces no dissatisfaction with this.

She gives two reasons for the way things have worked out, the second of which—succinct and direct, as she tends to be—is "I've got the boobs." The first reason is that she found the cry of a baby—her baby at the top of the list but babies she hears when she's walking down the street as well—almost physically painful. It's a sound that she *has* to address if in any way she possibly can.

As she said, she got the kid she got: Sofia was a picky eater and a restless sleeper; she had colic; she had reflux; she was often in pain; she cried *a lot*. And, for the first three years of her life, nursing was virtually the only reliably effective, if temporary, solution to her crying.

Andrea would have liked to have nursed for a shorter period of time; she would have liked *not* to have been the default parent on call in the middle of the night and into the small hours of the early morning; Darryl would have liked to have done more—it was a matter of some personal pain and frustration to him that he could not comfort and soothe his daughter during that period.

He didn't have the breasts.

As every parent knows, when you are out and around with a child, you don't have the kind of personal space accorded most adults: *Everyone* is suddenly licensed to give you advice about the most intimate issues. From family, from friends, from strangers on the street, you get a constant chorus—sometimes well intentioned, sometimes forceful to the point of anger—of suggestions and commandments about how you should be treating your child.

Three years is a long time to nurse a child.[3]

Too long?

"Most kids don't breast-feed for three years, right?" Andrea acknowledges.

They *did* try giving her a bottle, Andrea says, in part to give *her* a break, in part to allow Darryl to do feedings; she pumped breast milk from Day Two.

"She did get [bottle fed]," Andrea says. "But she would cry and I couldn't stand it. It was physically agony for me to hear her cry.[4] And I would be like, *give the child to me or I'm going to kill*—I mean it was like that. . . . She cried from five in the evening until three in the morning. And the only thing, ultimately, that seemed to calm her—until it *wouldn't* calm her—was the boob."

This had an early impact on how parenting was divided up.

"I had the comfort ticket," Andrea says, "so that meant that I ended up playing more of a dominant role than *I* wanted. *I* didn't want to be the last resort for every damn thing that ever went wrong!"

As much as this was a barrier to Darryl's taking a more nurturing role with his daughter, he still took on a good deal of what needed to be done around the house.

"The bottom line when I was breast-feeding," Andrea says, "is I had to do the breast-feeding, he had to do everything else: He needed to do the laundry; he needed to do the cooking; he needed to take out the garbage; he needed to take the dog for a walk."

Of course, she recalls, they got no small amount of advice about this situation.

"Like *let her cry; let her be,*" Andrea remembers being told. "And my response was, 'No, you don't understand. She isn't just crying. She's screaming. It's agony for her. It doesn't stop after forty-five minutes; it goes on and on for hours and hours and hours.' I couldn't do it [let her cry it out]."

As an ideological matter, Andrea doesn't subscribe to the "biology as destiny" model; she's not an essentialist. But she does pay attention to the evidence of her own experience. Most—though not all—of the women she knows have a similar response to a child in distress, a *need* to respond that feels like it has a physical dimension to it. She knows *some* men who respond as well—Darryl included. But she characterizes this as more a matter of learning or training or conscious effort, whereas she sees the reaction of women as something far more visceral—something else written in the body, whether we see that writing as experiential or biological.

We *learn* family, she argues, as children, as a set of reflexes, beliefs, practices, rituals. Both for men and for women, early experience forms the core of how we approach parenthood ourselves.

Some of us come at the question of how to set up our families by negation, making good on the childhood cry that *I'm never going to do that when I have kids!*

When we lose a parent in childhood, however—whether to illness, death, or divorce—we lose a fundamental guidepost. It's much easier to conform to or react against something that's actually there; it's much more difficult to project into the void.

We have a range of other models to look at, of course—extended family, friends, media images—but none of those have the same impact as immersion in our own families, day after day, year after year. You learn baseball—or any sport for that matter—by playing and playing and playing, by etching those reflexes into your body. What you move toward on the field, what you move away from, the sounds, the sensations, the muscle-memory, that's what guides you, not abstract notions or disembodied information.

Reading the sports section, watching TV, or going to games can take you only so far.

Pregnant Men

"I've felt pretty comfortable being in the culture of the caregivers," Darryl says. "I see more and more guys in the park with strollers; I think it's much more accepted."

Andrea's take is shaded in a slightly different direction.

"Generally," she says, "I think it's not easy for men to talk about themselves as parents, *in the world*."

She does see progress in some of the spaces that she refers to as *Parentland*. As Darryl said, there are more men in the park with children; Andrea notes an increase in fathers at school meetings and functions; when the focus is children, she says, more and more men are able to open up.

She doesn't think things have opened up as much in all-male environments, especially for men who are stay-at-home dads.

"You can talk about the office or about sports scores," she says, "but not *my kid isn't sleeping at night*. Everything stops. Suddenly they feel bad because that's not happening with them, but with their wives."

The difference between what they say is notable, perhaps in part a product of Darryl's idealizing his circumstances and of Andrea's being blunt.

But the situation she describes could just as easily be a conversation among professional women, brought to an uncomfortable pause by a stay-at-home mom in their midst launching into a discussion of the problems she's having with her children.

Are the parents who stay at home with their children—out of choice or out of necessity—doing something noble or "avoiding work" and taking on lesser challenges?

Are the parents who work outside the home shirking their familial obligations or admirably embracing personal and professional advancement?

Role Confusion—*Who am I supposed to be and how am I supposed to represent myself?*—is an equal opportunity problem. We're unlikely to solve it anytime soon: Most of us juggle multiple identities. Addressing the problem more directly, however, would benefit a broad swath of people: mothers as well as fathers, parents who work outside the home as well as stay-at-home parents.

Warren's "father-shaped hole in the soul," this spiritual and emotional loss made concrete, is also an *experiential* loss, a loss of lessons learned.

How do we make up for that?

A piece of Darryl's response is the actor's exuberance and the realtor's boosterism—essentially: *Move to Seattle!*

The more measured response, perhaps, is *Choose to raise your family in a cultural environment that supports the kinds of choices you want to make*—admittedly, the three-word slogan is a little easier to commit to memory.

Darryl had significant expectations for himself as a parent; Andrea had expectations for him as well. But the fact that the local culture ratified and reinforced those expectations was also key.

It's been almost twenty years since he lived on the East Coast, so it's hard for him to assess what might constitute national, broader, social change and what might be more a matter of local culture. But he cites Seattle as one of the places that has been on the cutting edge of a kind of *Back to the Future* birth movement. Home births, midwifery, doulas,[5] and birth coaches are becoming more the norm than an exception, he says.

Making birth more of a human, rather than medical, event, emphasizing the role of family over the role of professionals, has made more space for fathers as active parents.

Darryl suggests a number of factors that have done something to open up parenting to men and that have supported him in the ongoing struggle to be the kind of father he wants to be. Much of this, he points out, starts before our children are born, with childbirth preparation and parenting classes that an increasing number of men take alongside their wives, for example.

There is a growing library of books aimed directly at men who are "expectant fathers."

"*Pregnant Fathers* was a big one for me," Darryl says of books that impacted his thinking. "That book was *huge* for me in terms of helping me understand that *I'm in this too, this is about me too.*"

"Think about the number of [similar] books out there," he continues. "Even if I didn't read all of them, Andrea read them and I got the CliffsNotes version."

He also notes that both the stereotype and the reality of what happens on maternity wards have changed substantially over time: In our grandparents' day, men were often chased—or voluntarily exiled themselves—as far away from the birth process as possible; in our fathers' day, the iconic image was the man pacing in the waiting room, cigars at the ready; Darryl and I are not unusual in our generation in that we were in the birthing room and actively involved—both of us cut our daughters' umbilical cords, for example: We were *there.*

Parenting hasn't worked out exactly how either Darryl or Andrea expected it to. But they have found ways to take care of each other and to take care of their daughter with which they are both satisfied.

Both of them felt that they missed out on childhood experiences of their own that would have better prepared them to be parents. But they have found the resources, the strength, and the persistence to make up these deficits.

We may, as Andrea believes, carry our histories, our personal narratives, our stories, inscribed in our bodies—sometimes a joy, sometimes a burden. But as Darryl's relationship with both his father and his daughter demonstrate, with enough focus and intentionality, with an eye on the past as well as the future, we also have the ability to rewrite these narratives, to learn both to represent ourselves and to live our lives in relation to others in more complete and more satisfying ways.

6

· · · · · · · ·

Poppins versus Kramer:
Dad, You Have *Really* Changed!

· · · · · · · ·

Ted: I'm not that late.
Billy: Wanna bet? All the other mothers were here
before you.

—From the movie *Kramer vs. Kramer,* 1979

The movies *Mary Poppins* and *Kramer vs. Kramer* more or less bookend my childhood: The first came out in 1964, two years after I was born; the second came out in 1979, the year after my parents got divorced. They are of interest to me in part for that reason; they are images I grew up with. But they are also enduring classics: Whether you like or loathe *Mary Poppins,* the movie is part of the very air we breathe.[1] Whether you respect or disdain *Kramer vs. Kramer,* it was nominated for nine Academy Awards and won five, including Best Picture; moreover, it put modern single fathers on the map.

What do these movies show us about what men are capable of, how men have changed or could change, what it means to be a father?

These questions probably sound a little odd applied to the first movie. Either as a parent or as an ex-child, you *know Mary Poppins,* the book and/or the movie—the trademark umbrella-wielding British nanny, the dancing, the magic, the wacky fun—and it's not about fathers. It's about children.[2]

Except you *don't* know the movie—particularly if you haven't seen it since childhood.

Any time I have students watch *Mary Poppins* and critically analyze it, they come away shocked; it isn't anything like what they remember.

In Lit Crit 101,[3] we pound into our students the idea that stories have to have dramatic conflict at their core. The classic story arc involves that conflict sparking change, usually in one or more of the central characters. I'll return to the book in a moment, but let's start with the film, since that is my main focus here. What do most of us remember about *Mary Poppins*, the movie?

Well, there are those sweet but slightly difficult children, right? And they're not very happy, and they're not really behaving well, and their parents are a bit distracted, and Mary Poppins floats in on a stiff breeze and puts all things domestic in proper order. She makes the kids happy and then floats off again, right? And there's singing and dancing and everyone who isn't Julie Andrews is probably Dick Van Dyke—who plays the versatile Bert, sometime bard of the park, chalk picture artist, and chimney sweep, among other roles.

Good enough as far as it goes. Indeed she puts the household right. *How?*

What changes?

What we most often remember is that the children's *circumstances* are changed. But the *character* who undergoes the most radical change over the course of the film is the father—with the mother a distant second. And, although one rather doubts that this is what the "high concept pitch" to Walt Disney himself sounded like, we can compress the story into this somewhat odd sentence: Magical nanny descends on middle-class household in Edwardian England and induces a psychotic break in the father, converting him from a cold and distant bureaucrat to a nurturing parent.

A Book, a Movie, a Nervous Breakdown

In P. L. Travers's 1934 book, the Banks family live in shabby gentility: Theirs is "the smallest house in the lane. And besides that, it is the only one that is rather dilapidated and needs a coat of paint."[4]

Mr. Banks told his wife, we are informed, that she could have either "a nice, clean, comfortable house or four children. But not both, for he couldn't afford it."[5]

This is a home, apparently—this is a relationship—in which husband and wife consult, discuss, and negotiate.

Mrs. Banks opts for kids over comfort, and, in the book, Jane and Michael are supplemented by the baby twins, John and Barbara.

In the movie, by way of contrast, the father starts out as a pompous and arrogant domestic dictator and the mother a somewhat daft suffragette. Neither is particularly plugged in to what is going on around them, least of all to their children.

Near the beginning of the movie, the children have run away from their nanny for the fourth time that week and the nanny, in response, has thrown up her hands and quit. It takes the other servants some time to penetrate Mrs. Banks's political fog, after she comes home from a fine day of disobedience both civil and uncivil, to make her understand the circumstances.

Then Mr. Banks comes home from his job at the bank, and she has to return the favor by trying to bring him up to speed. He's even more oblivious, lost in a fantasy of order and male authority. His first song sketches the world as he sees it, beginning with this stanza:

> It's grand to be an Englishman in 1910
> King Edward's on the throne
> It's *The Age of Men*
> I'm the lord of my castle
> The sovereign, the liege
> I treat my subjects—servants, children, wife
> With a firm but gentle hand
> *Noblesse oblige* . . . [6]

It's downhill from there for George Banks.

Mary Poppins arrives soon thereafter, and her entrance heralds a stunning decline in Mr. Banks's authority and his sense of self—not merely figuratively but literally. She completely flummoxes him: He bangs his head on the stone fireplace; he stammers; he momentarily forgets his own name and has to be reminded of it.

Mary Poppins accepts the job. She essentially hires herself—on her own terms, of course—and then proceeds to take the children on a series of adventures.

Mr. Banks disapproves and attempts to sternly lecture Mary Poppins about all this frivolity. But somehow he can't seem to get to or to hold the rhetorical high ground. She turns the conversation around, appearing to agree with him that the children need more serious activities to prepare them for what real life will be like, ultimately convincing him that *he* should therefore take the children on an outing, to see the bank where he works.

Unfortunately, Michael, the younger child, unwittingly causes a run on the bank, when he refuses to turn over his tuppence to the bank president for investment—"Welcome to our joyful family of investors!" the president says as he snatches the coin from the child's hand.

The bank's customers misconstrue Michael's cry "They won't give me back my money!" triggering panic and a near riot.

Fleeing the chaos in the bank, Jane and Michael tear through streets and back alleys menaced by an old woman who looks like a fairy tale witch and by a barking dog, teeth bared and salivating, and career right into Bert, this time kitted out as a chimney sweep.

Bert tries to calm them down, tells them he'll take care of them like he was their own father, and asks who's after them.

Their father, they tell him.

They have a quick exchange in which the children are brutally direct about how they think their father feels about them:

Bert: Well, now, there must be some mistake. Your dad's a fine gentleman and he loves ya!

Jane: I don't think so. You should've seen the look on his face.

Michael: He doesn't like us at all.

Bert: Well, now that don't seem likely, does it?

Jane: It's true.

The problem isn't just what has happened at the bank and it isn't "merely" that they don't believe their father loves them; they don't even think he *likes* them.

With interesting backspin, however, Bert's response is *not* to offer comfort by agreeing with the children or by expressing sympathy for *their* situation. Instead, he expresses sympathy for, and succinctly explains, the situation—the emotional predicament, really—of their father.

This is *not* the Mr. Banks of the book, who was largely absent but reasonably affectionate and reasonably reasonable when he was around, more a slightly befuddled foil for his family and his servants than any kind of serious authority figure.

Near the beginning of the book, when the family has just lost its nanny and is once again looking, Mrs. Banks complains about the way Katie Nanna left:

> "Without 'by your leave' or a word of warning. And what am I to do?" said Mrs. Banks.
>
> "Advertise, my dear," said Mr. Banks, putting on his shoes. "And I wish Robertson Ay [another of the servants] would go without a word of warning, for he has again polished one boot and left the other untouched. I shall look very lopsided."[7]

The emotionally repressed Mr. Banks—the Disney version—whom Bert accurately and poignantly describes is less the lovable, if mildly unplugged, father of the British books and more a harried and ambitious postwar *American* executive. We recognize him from books published in the mid-1950s that describe how routine and bureaucracy are destroying the souls of the modern American worker, books like William H. Whyte's 1956 classic, *The Organization Man*, or Sloan Wilson's *The Man in the Gray Flannel Suit*—published in 1955, turned into a movie starring Gregory Peck the following year.

The cinematic Mr. Banks, that is to say, evokes the failings and the foibles of neither the men of Edwardian England in which the movie is set nor of Georgian England, just before World War II, when *Mary Poppins* was first published, but rather the atmosphere of postwar

America, where questions were beginning to crop up about the down-side of the conformist 1950s. It's worth pointing out in this context that the movie's 1964 release date puts it a year after the 1963 publication of Betty Friedan's *The Feminine Mystique*, which deconstructed the 1950s from the point of view of gender relations.

Bert: Let's sit down. You know, begging your pardon, but the one my heart goes out to is your father. There he is in that cold, heartless bank day after day, hemmed in by mounds of cold, heartless money. I don't like to see any living thing caged up.

Jane: Father in a cage?

Bert: They makes cages in all sizes and shapes, you know. Bank-shaped some of 'em, carpets and all.

Jane: Father's not in trouble. We are.

Bert: Oh, sure about that, are you? Look at it this way. You've got your mother to look after you. And Mary Poppins, and Constable Jones and me. Who looks after your father? Tell me that. When something terrible happens, what does he do? Fends for himself, he does. Who does he tell about it? No one! Don't blab his troubles at home. He just pushes on at his job, uncomplaining and alone and silent.

Michael: He's not very silent!

Jane: Michael, be quiet. Bert, do you think Father really needs our help?

Bert: Well, not my place to say. I only observe that a father can always do with a bit of help. Come on, I'll take you home.

Note that the list of people Bert gives, on whom the children can rely, consists entirely of either women or working-class men; Bert has said that their father loves them, but their father doesn't make the list. Note the hierarchy as well: The women come first, Mother at the top of the list, though Mary Poppins is the more active "mother"; title trumps actions.

The upshot of *Take Your Kids to Work Day* is that Mr. Banks is fired.

More than just losing his job, he loses his identity, losing his name for the second time in the movie—the first time he forgot it himself; this time it is taken away by force. He is *De-Banked*, drummed out in the manner of a disgraced officer being ejected from the armed forces, his banker's uniform sundered in the same way that officers—in movies, at any rate—have the epaulets torn from their shoulders: a fist thrust through his bowler hat, his umbrella turned inside out, the petals torn from the flower in his lapel.

What can one do in such a situation?

He snaps.

And the word he cries to soothe his pain is "Supercalifragilisticexpialidocious!" one of Mary Poppins's incantations.

It *does* make him feel better, and he skips out of the bank, shouting the word and laughing uncontrollably, disappearing into the night.

That's one good way to get out of a prison—however well carpeted it may be—don't just plead. *Demonstrate* insanity.

When he hasn't returned home the following morning, the family is concerned that he may have killed himself. He's a man, after all: No Job = No Life.

When he reappears, he is holding his children's kite, newly repaired by his own hand,[8] and sporting a new attitude as well. Mrs. Banks donates her suffragist sash as the kite's tail, and they head off to the park as a family.

If we stop there, Mr. Banks is jobless but happy. His wife appears to have cast aside her silly notions of equality—having torn off and donated her sash to the cause of family; he has had his banker's uniform torn off involuntarily. In short, both parents are connected to their children in a way we haven't seen before in the movie.

You could say that they lived carefree ever after. We walk to the brink of an interesting sociocultural precipice, the father radicalized—letting go of his job and tight-lipped personality, connecting with his children—bookended paradoxically by his wife letting go of her more unconventional notions.

In the park, however, they encounter a good deal of the cast of the movie, including the bank's board of trustees, all flying kites.

It turns out Mr. Banks's psychotic episode had such an effect on the bank president that he "died laughing," which has spurred his son and his colleagues to take a day off to celebrate and has lightened them all up to the point that they conclude that Mr. Banks is such a fine fellow that he deserves not merely his job back but promotion to the board of trustees as well. Just in the nick of time, Disney pulls us back from the brink and back into the bank—a better bank now, it would appear, but still . . .

So it *is* possible to be a good father, to break out of your business suit and head to the park with your children. You just have to be out of your mind to take the first steps—and sometimes you need a little magical nudge and a *deus ex machina*.

In the final scene, just before Mary Poppins flies away, we pull back from the crowd in the park to watch her, as she watches the family from the Banks' front stoop. She has a brief dialogue with the talking bird's head that is her umbrella handle, again ratifying that her purpose was to change the father and that her purpose has been achieved.

Her words are firm; her eyes water just a little.

Umbrella: That's gratitude for you. Didn't even say good-bye.

Mary Poppins: No, they didn't.

Umbrella: Look at them. You know, they think more of their father than they do of you.

Mary Poppins: That's as it should be.

Umbrella: Well, don't you care?

Mary Poppins: Practically perfect people never permit sentiment to muddle their thinking.

Umbrella: Is that so? Well, I'll tell you one thing, Mary Poppins, you don't fool me a bit.

Mary Poppins: Oh, really?

Umbrella: Yes, really. I know exactly how you feel about these children. And if you think I'm gonna keep my mouth shut any longer, I—

Mary Poppins (*pinching its beak shut*): That will be quite enough of that, thank you.

The twinning in *Mary Poppins* of insanity with male nurturance has deep roots in fiction, and we see it in a broad range of movies from the 1980s to the present: from *Mr. Mom* (in which losing his job and becoming a househusband destabilize Michael Keaton) to *Mrs. Doubtfire* (in which Robin Williams is "forced" to cross-dress to stay close to his children), from *Paternity* (Arnold Schwarzenegger gets pregnant and irrational) to *Unstrung Heroes* (the uncles that are a young boy's emotional life preservers are unstable to the point that one of them is committed to a mental institution).

This association has deep roots in many cultures as well. The word "hysteria," after all, comes from the Greek word *hyster* meaning "womb," hysteria having originally been thought to be caused by an agitation of the uterus, which some ancient physicians believed took to drifting around the body, causing mischief. This connection is by no means restricted to fiction, and the deploying of accusations of insanity against people who buck the mainstream is not something that happens only in Stalinist Russia.

In Chapter 9 I look at the case of former Maryland state trooper and helicopter paramedic Kevin Knussman. He was the first person to file a lawsuit alleging gender discrimination under the federal Family and Medical Leave Act, when he was refused a leave to take care of his ailing wife and newborn daughter.

How did the Maryland State Police respond?

Among other things, apparently believing that Kevin had been deranged by his concern for family, they pronounced him psychiatrically unfit and grounded him.

Where's Mary Poppins when we need her most?

Ted Kramer and the Other Mothers

Ted Kramer (Dustin Hoffman) isn't *nudged* into the role of primary parent; he's thrown headlong, in the opening beats of *Kramer vs. Kramer*.[9] He comes home late from the office, clearly a regular occurrence, and his wife Joanna (Meryl Streep) is waiting for him, suitcase in hand.

Here are my keys, my credit cards, my checkbook, and she is out the door and gone, their son, Billy (Justin Henry), asleep in his bedroom, the walls a skyscape spattered with the clouds that she painted for him. The child awakens the next morning to a radically altered domestic landscape; he is in the care of an instant single father.

Hoffman's character stumbles at first, of course. It's clear that he hasn't had much experience taking care of his son, in either a practical or an emotional sense. We watch him find his stride, watch him learn, watch him change; like Kevin Hill, we essentially watch him redeem himself. His neighbor Margaret (Jane Alexander), another single parent, becomes his closest—though strictly platonic—confidante; he doesn't *look* for a replacement mother, he *becomes* the replacement mother. My use of language, of course, is wholly intentional.

He loses his job because of the time he has to devote to taking care of Billy. Professional women complain about "hitting the glass ceiling" and being unable to rise beyond a certain level in their careers. Ted has the *floor* beneath him turn to glass and falls through it, into a lower-paying job.

His wife returns, sues for custody, and wins. In the final scene of the movie, however, (spoiler alert!) she finds herself emotionally unable to remove Billy from his father's care.

Chalk one up for the power of positive fathering.

Every Text a Rorschach Test

We bring all the knowledge, logic, and finesse we can to analyzing any text, any cultural artifact. We strive for—at the very least the appearance of—fairness and accuracy. But, in the end, to one degree or another, every text is an ink blot.

"What this text tells us" is a way of saying, "what *I* see," which is inevitably, sometimes embarrassingly, a way of saying, "Let me reveal something about myself here."

As a personal matter, *Kramer vs. Kramer* touched me—*continues* to touch me—in areas where I remain emotionally raw into my midforties. In the Introduction, I mentioned my daughter's question about a song on the radio: Had the example of the father in the song influenced the kind of parent I wanted to be and the kind of parent I wanted to avoid being?

Of course it had.

Culture matters—particularly the cultural models we are exposed to during childhood and adolescence.

Ted Kramer was a particularly vivid example for me in a number of ways, some of them contradictory, not all of them positive: I admire what the character does; I am angered—still—by what is done *to* the character.

When cultures are in flux, rules become more fluid as well. The questioning of gender roles that accelerated in the 1960s—and is ongoing today—cast a broad variety of rules into doubt. Many have yet to cohere into a new consensus; it isn't clear that some ever will.

Dating provides a somewhat less complex example than parenting issues. Traditionally, men were expected to pay for dinner. This was part of a chivalric ethic; it also reflected the economic inequality between the sexes. By the time I started dating, in the 1970s, that norm had started to fray around the edges. But no clear standard had yet emerged and—some thirty-five years later—we arguably *still* don't have a broadly accepted answer to the question of who pays for dinner.

As I have already written, overall I am in favor of the fracturing of those older norms; they were, in many ways, oppressive. Now that they are gone—or, at any rate, no longer hold a monopoly on how we are to behave—I understand and accept that we have to do a lot more overt negotiating over how we structure a variety of relationships, from how we deal with dating to how we deal with our children.

What upsets me is when I feel that these negotiations are used as a cloak for gaining personal advantage under the guise of loftier discussions; what *angers* me is when such arguments are fluid to the point of hypocrisy.

In the "Who pays?" example, there are a variety of answers that I find reasonable, from "The person who proffers the invitation," to "Both," to "We alternate." I am less receptive to the "Gentlemen always pay" argument. If the woman making that argument didn't have the wherewithal to pay, that would be reasonable; if she were a traditionalist through and through, playing the chivalry card would at least be consistent. If she were unsure, wrestling with the question, fair enough; we all are. If, however, her consistent orientation was in the direction of "equality" when that meant benefit for her and a quick reversion to "tradition" whenever equality might cost her something—literally or figuratively—that has always struck me as manipulative.

I will accept being told that I am insufficiently egalitarian, when I fail to discuss or negotiate enough.

I will accept being called rude, for failing to be deferential or sufficiently sensitive—although I often suspect that the button being pushed there, albeit covertly, has more to do with the rather more vexed category of chivalry.

To be called both, to be slapped on both cheeks simultaneously, I find infuriating.

What do you want *from me!* is my reflexive response.

That's how I see Ted Kramer.

He starts out an insensitive workaholic, and this costs him his marriage; the dramatic arc of the movie is his evolution into a caring and sensitive parent—explicitly sacrificing professional goals in favor of taking care of his child.

His reward?

He loses custody of his son—in part because fathers can't compete with mothers as parents, but also in part because he has become insufficiently focused on what men are supposed to be focused on: work.

"He pretends to fitness," his ex-wife's lawyer tells the court, "when he cannot hold a job."

What do we want *from him!*

It is true that he regains custody of the child in the last ninety seconds of the movie. But this is an extralegal matter, an act of grace (*perhaps*—we can parse her motivations a little later) on the part of his wife. As a matter of law, as a matter of the official functioning of the state, of family court, the apparatus set up to certify what constitutes "the best interests of the child," he loses. He has not done enough to move the scales of justice. And given the effort we've seen him make, it's hard to imagine what could possibly *be* sufficient.

When is it that a man in his circumstances can be construed to have done enough?

I am moved by the ultimate father-and-child reunion. The tenuousness of that last-minute save, however, hits a raw nerve for me, more a reminder of the precariousness of the father-child relationship than of its strength.

Hoffman versus Kramer

The movie *Kramer vs. Kramer* was socially relevant when it came out and has been socially resonant ever since; I present support for this position a little farther on. What I want to do first, however—having sketched something of what the movie means to me—is to look at the genesis of the story, how the project evolved, the role that author, producer, director, screenwriter, and actors had in forming and re-forming the narrative. Ascribing motives and intentions to writers, actors, and directors is a dicey business; I will stick as closely as I can here to verifiable information and clear public statements.

The novel *Kramer vs. Kramer* was published in 1977. Delving into divorce and child custody issues was not the point for author Avery Corman; rather it was a means to an end. In December 1979, shortly after the movie's release, Michael Kernan published an article in the *Washington Post*, entitled "Fathering of a Hit: 'Kramer' vs. Corman; Corman's 'Kramer'; The Author's Praise of Paternity."

> "We took the boys to see the movie of 'Kramer vs. Kramer,' and it was mind-boggling" [the article begins, quoting Corman]. "I couldn't talk. I tried to ask [my son] Nickie what he thought of it, but I literally couldn't get the words out. Because he and his brother—they were what it was about."
>
> Avery Corman is not divorced. He and his wife, Judy, have been married 12 years,[10] and their kids are now 8 and 5, and

he is delighted when somebody thinks his book, *Kramer vs. Kramer*, is about his own life.

"It's very flattering," he says. "It means I've been able to communicate what I felt."

What he felt was very simple: the silent, proud, fierce, and achingly shy love of a father for his child.

"That was my starting point, what it was like to be a daddy. Then I developed it: What if something happened, if the family broke up . . . ?"[11]

What Corman wanted to write about was a nurturing father. He didn't feel that he could do that in dramatically effective fashion—that the father in his story would have sufficient space to define and reveal himself, particularly in relation to his son—if the mother were still present. In the book, Joanna Kramer isn't so much malign as she is weak and selfish; at the end, she relinquishes custody not for Billy's sake but because she is too unstable to be a responsible parent. There is no final scene either between exes or between mother and child. Rather, Joanna telephones instead.

"'I mean . . . sitting in the courtroom . . . hearing what you've done . . . what's involved . . .' He could barely make out her words. 'The responsibilities . . .'"[12]

Producer Stanley Jaffe bought the movie rights to the book and signed on Robert Benton to do a screen adaptation and to direct, and they set about casting the film. They wanted Dustin Hoffman for the role of Ted Kramer. Jaffe had pictured Hoffman in the role as soon as he bought the property; Benton immediately agreed.[13] There was only one small obstacle.

Hoffman didn't want the part.

When Benton and Jaffe went to England in 1977, to meet with Hoffman—who was shooting a movie there—and discuss the role, Hoffman's reticence was such that he was waiting for them in the hotel lobby when they arrived for the meeting; he didn't want to invite them up to his suite; he didn't want to get into an extended discussion; he just wanted to dispose of the matter as quickly as possible.

The hotel bar was full, however, not a table to be had, and Hoffman had to acquiesce.

"On such things hang amazing consequences," Benton said.

Hoffman had some artistic issues with the script. But his core problem with *Kramer vs. Kramer* was personal. At the time of this meeting, Hoffman had recently separated from his family, from Anne Byrne, his wife of eight years; her daughter, Karina; and their daughter, Jenna. Their divorce was finalized in 1980.[14]

Hoffman says he told Jaffe and Benton, "What I am experiencing [in his own divorce] is just so different, and so much deeper than what I read of the novel and what I read in your screenplay. I'm not connecting with it, and because it's something I'm going through, I think it would be too painful for me."

They ended up cutting a deal. Hoffman agreed to play the part, as long as he could participate in the process of shaping the screenplay into one that felt sufficiently real to him, sufficiently true to what he was experiencing.[15]

Hoffman had recently moved out of his family's Manhattan townhouse and bought a co-op overlooking Central Park with an extra bedroom for the children. He split his time between there and a house he was leasing in Los Angeles.[16] Jaffe moved into the Carlyle Hotel, a block off the park on the East Side, and he, Hoffman, and Benton embarked on a series of twelve-hour days of talking, arguing, and writing.

Jaffe says it was "almost like group therapy."

Between January and September of 1978, they produced at least four drafts.[17]

Both Benton and Jaffe wanted the film to show the unvarnished truth of divorce, not to facilely take sides. Streep was given latitude to flesh out and better humanize Joanna's character—among other things, rewriting one of the crucial courtroom speeches that her character makes. Hoffman stresses that, in his view, one of the core tragedies of divorce is not the death of love, but its painful and inconvenient persistence: We would like to be able to turn off, to be done with various emotions, as and after we extricate ourselves from relationships, but the heart is rarely that predictable or cooperative.

As an objective, structural matter—in the movie version—both Joanna and Ted are redeemed, and they are redeemed by the same act: Both of them change; both of them rise above their own personal concerns; both of them are willing to give up their son to save their son.

It's King Solomon and the baby—except, in the end, no one gives the wrong answer.

Writing in his review of the movie, in the *Chicago Sun-Times*, on December 1, 1979, Roger Ebert opens with "*Kramer vs. Kramer* wouldn't be half as good as it is—half as intriguing and absorbing—if the movie had taken sides."[18]

Benton argues that the audience has good reason to cheer for Joanna.

"She is the one who does the final, totally heroic act," he says. "She doesn't give up Billy . . . because she *doesn't* love him, but because she *does* love him."

For all of that, my identification is with Ted, both his love for his child and his anger at his wife. Some of that, as I've sketched earlier, is *my* baggage, but some of it is also Hoffman's. He did an impressive job of portraying the pain and anger that a man feels on going through a divorce, because he *was* a man going through a divorce.

"I am sure I was acting out on her [Streep], throughout the movie," he has said, "stuff that I was feeling toward the wife that I was divorcing in real life."

He and Ted blend.

At a crucial point in the movie, Joanna has come back after eighteen months, and has invited Ted out for a drink to tell him that she is going to pursue custody of Billy. They shoot the scene multiple times and Hoffman tells Benton that he doesn't feel that it's working.

"I'm really angry by the end—I just, I know that I just don't, I don't, I, I just—I am really *pissed*," his upset still manifest in the chaos of his language when he talks about this more than twenty years later.

Benton and Streep know that Hoffman is going to try something different on the final take—the take they end up using—but they don't know what that is. On getting up to leave, he takes a half step away and then bats his wine glass—not a prop—against the wall, smashing it right next to Streep.

His feelings are indistinguishable from Ted's. Smashing the glass, Hoffman says, "felt wonderful."

Daddy's Home?

Kramer vs. Kramer was *not* simply a fantasy about how parenthood *might* change, about what men *might* be like if they were active parents; it reflected an increasingly sharp focus on the figure of the engaged father as key to a healthy society—at a time when both divorce and the dual-earner household were becoming increasingly common.

The flip side of this dynamic is the 1965 Moynihan Report, "The Negro Family: The Case for National Action," issued by the U.S. Department of Labor, in which the social and economic problems of the African American community were ascribed to an epidemic of missing fathers, which had led to what future U.S. Senator Daniel Patrick Moynihan referred to as a pathological matriarchy.[19]

At the same time that the number of households headed by single mothers was on the rise, however, so was the number of households headed by single fathers. The ratio in 1968 was approximately ten to one; by the year 2006, the ratio was closer to five to one.[20]

The matter of single-parent households is at a problematic nexus between race, gender, politics, class, morality, and economics—just to name a few hot buttons it either firmly pushes or dangerously grazes. In the most neutral terms: (1) Single-parent households have fewer resources than two-parent households, and (2) children raised in more resource-rich environments do better both economically and socially.

But this discussion contains little, if any, neutral ground.

In liberal circles, there has been a long-running argument about the degree to which focusing on family structure is a way to "blame the poor for being poor"[21] and to let the larger society off the hook for racism both past and present. While broad agreement exists in the African American community that absentee fathers are a serious problem, publicly airing this dirty laundry often provokes a strong backlash.

And for some feminists and other progressives, what constitutes a "healthy society" or "stronger family structure" is a vexed question—particularly when the prescription seems to be an increased male presence—redolent of an attempt to reassert patriarchal control.

Kramer vs. Kramer came out at a pivotal and statistically significant moment. According to the U.S. Census Bureau, between 1979 and 1980, the number of children living in a single-parent household headed by a father passed the one million mark. That's a trend that has both continued and accelerated.[22]

Ted Kramer's hold on the American imagination can be explained in part as an exercise in wish fulfillment, balm for the psychic scar of the absent father. If you want to make popular movies, you "give people what they want to see." In 1979, from a variety of points on the political and cultural spectrum, people wanted to see some real reordering of domestic arrangements.

Flash forward to 2006, and the aura of wish fulfillment begins to look more like prophesy. Neither my friend Darryl nor I—both children of divorce, both raised in part by single parents, both active fathers—have structured our family lives as we have in direct response to the cultural artifacts that surrounded us as we were growing up, but again, it bears repeating, the stories we tell ourselves about who we are have real consequences in terms of our ability to imaginatively project new social roles, both for ourselves and for our families.

An additional benchmark of the importance of *Kramer vs. Kramer* is the degree to which the movie has become a durable part of the on-going discussion of family structure and of parenting roles.

Some three years after the movie's release, in February 1982, film critic Molly Haskell excoriated the movie in a "Hers" column in the *New York Times*—I quote her in some detail later in this chapter—prompting a response in the form of a letter from a reader the following month. Another letter-writer in the *Times*, a year later, complaining about gender bias in custody decisions, contextualizes his complaint by writing, "Even in this post–'Kramer vs. Kramer' era, these days when there is an expectation of equality of the sexes before the law, courts are still cranking out the same old kind of custody justice they always have: give the kids to the woman and make the man pay."

A *Christian Science Monitor* piece in 1985, "Raising a Child Alone: A Task More Men Are Seeking,"[23] does a lead-in on *Kramer vs. Kramer*. Another opinion column in the *New York Times*, in 1989, "Daddy's Little Girl, Up to Date,"[24] does the same. *People Weekly* cites the movie in 1994,[25] quoting Betty Friedan. Reference to the movie crops up again in a *New York Times Sunday Magazine* "About Men" column in 1995.[26]

In 1996, the movie is used to examine the position of lawyers in popular culture, in an article in the *University of San Francisco Law Review* entitled "Peace between the Sexes: Law and Gender in *Kramer vs. Kramer*."[27] In 1998, the movie even forms the backbone of a piece in the British business journal *Management Today*, in which it is explained that the transformative experience that Ted Kramer underwent really centered on learning about what is referred to as "Total Quality Parenting," lessons easily transposed, the author argues, to the arena of office management.[28] The movie is also the linchpin of a 1999 article in *HR Magazine*, a human resources journal, entitled, "The Daddy Track."[29]

Into the twenty-first century, the movie remains alive in the consciousness of an eclectic, even global, swath of people, with references to it in *Women's Studies International Forum* (2001), in an article by a professor at the University of Delhi in India;[30] in *Culture and Organization* (2002);[31] and in *Cinema Journal* (2004),[32] in an article written by a professor at the University of Copenhagen—to name just a few.

You Are What You're Called

As I argue in Chapter 2, the ways the language of parenting has changed, and the ways it has resisted change, tell us a lot about how we see different roles. How the words "mother," "father," "parent," and "home" are deployed is pivotal in *Kramer vs. Kramer*. One point the movie makes very clear is that, in the late 1970s at least, the word "father" was insufficiently malleable, that it could not be expanded to include the idea of nurturing behavior. As Ted becomes a more involved parent—and consequently a better parent—he is rapidly converted into a "mother."

Sometimes this tagging is completely overt. About twenty-six minutes into the movie, for example, while Ted is still clearly in transition, he is late picking Billy up at a birthday party—echoes of the kind of inattention that destroyed his relationship with his wife.

"I'm not that late," he says defensively.

"Wanna bet?" Billy shoots back. "All the other mothers were here before you."

Ted attempts to defend himself against the charge of lateness; he makes no response to being called a mother.

Some ten minutes later, in further evidence of change, a similar scene is repeated.

Ted is on the couch, being yelled at by the boss.

It's been eight months, he's told, and he's getting worse.

"I can't let your family problems interfere," the boss says. "I've got a[n advertising] shop to run."

Ted assures him that it "won't happen again."

The phone rings; it's Billy, to talk to Ted.

From Ted's side of the conversation, we infer that they are arguing about the amount of TV that Billy can watch.

Ted responds, "I don't care what the other mothers do, Billy, we made a deal."

"I'm getting very nervous," the boss says, listening to this exchange, which ratifies for him that Ted is moving farther and farther away from reliable male breadwinner and closer and closer to unreliable—Mommy Track—employee.

Note that in the first instance, it is Billy who calls Ted a mother; in the second instance, it is Ted himself who uses the word, granted that he is obviously echoing his son (from which we can infer that the boy's usage is more or less habitual). We are also given the information in this scene that "it's been eight months [since his wife left]." She returns after fifteen months; so we can see that Ted's transformation of self-identity is all but complete more or less at the midpoint in his wife's absence.

In at least two other instances, Ted's identification as a mother is made more subtly and circumstantially, either through visual representation or through implication.

In a scene that almost immediately follows the office scene, we see Billy in a Halloween play, with Ted in the audience. Billy is having trouble with his lines, which Ted is reciting aloud in sync. At one point, Ted calls out the appropriate lines to Billy. Throughout this scene, when we pull back from close-ups of Ted, we see that the eight seats immediately surrounding him—one on either side, the row of three in front of him and the row of three behind him, the only ones that we can see—are all occupied by women, presumably the mothers and the grandmothers of the children on stage.

Another scene in which Ted is put physically into "a mother's space" takes place in a hospital emergency room. Billy has fallen off a jungle gym in Central Park and cut his face, while Ted and Margaret are talking on a nearby bench. Ted runs several blocks to the emergency room, with the bleeding child in his arms. Margaret follows a few minutes later, entering as the doctor is completing his assessment. She stays in the room with Billy while Ted and the doctor step outside to consult. The doctor says that Billy is going to need ten stitches or so and suggests Ted wait outside while this is done.

"You just step over here," he says. "There's no reason for you to be in there."

"Yeah there is," Ted responds hotly. "He's my son. If you're going to do something to him, I'm going to be with him."[33]

This statement is notable not only for its vehemence but for the fact that Ted's central failing, as both a father and a husband, has previously been his absence, both physical and emotional. His words tell us that—of course!—he will be there for his son. The emphatic manner in which he delivers them ratifies that he now finds it inconceivable that anyone would think he could act any other way, that is to say, the way he acted for most of his son's life, previous to his wife's departure.

The background for this conversation, moreover, both visual and aural, is Billy lying on a stretcher, his face covered with blood, crying, "Stay, Daddy, stay! Daddy, stay!"

Emotionally hurt by having been abandoned by his mother, he is now physically hurt and terrified of being abandoned by his father: Joanna left; Ted stays.

Interestingly, Margaret's presence in the ER is not questioned at all: As a woman—the doctors may infer that she is the child's mother; no one asks—it is assumed that she is acting "appropriately" in seeking to physically comfort a wounded child. Ted on the other hand is not merely deemed irrelevant in this situation; rather, his presence is actively labeled inappropriate. Yet by this time he has changed so much that he contests this and inserts himself into the same physical space that Margaret occupies brooking no critical questioning, as if by right. In effect, he asserts his parental (or paternal) right to be present, by claiming a space that has been marked by the other participants as maternal.

In the scene that immediately follows this, we find Margaret in Ted's kitchen, drying dishes, after Ted has put Billy to bed. She is guilt ridden about what has happened—which parallels Ted's feelings; they are both suffering a kind of mother-guilt over the accident. Ted comforts her in part by segueing into a request that she take care of the child if some serious misfortune should happen to Ted ("like if a building were to fall on me," he says, which gives an indication of how serious a misfortune would have to be now to come between him and his son).

"If something were to happen to me," he asks, "would you take care of Billy? I can't think of anyone else that I would trust with him. You're a good mother."

Here, Ted's identity as a "mother" is reinforced in the sense that his credibility in recognizing Margaret as "a good mother" is predicated on his own discovery of how to be "a good mother," evoking both practical experience and a kind of tribal bond.

The Legal Power of "Motherhood"

For millennia, in common law—first Roman, then English—a father's right to custody was absolute. He could sell his children if he so chose. In the United States, after the Civil War, the movement to win women *sui juris* status—the right to testify in court, to inherit, to divorce, to own property independently of husbands or fathers, for example—included the right of child custody. By the beginning of the twentieth century, the "tender years doctrine" overwhelmingly favored women over men in custody decisions. Fast-forward to 1979, the year that *Kramer vs. Kramer* was released, and things are beginning to change again. That same year, California passed the first joint custody law. By the early 1990s, more than forty states had such statutes, making joint custody either an option or an outright preference under the law.[34]

The custody battle, which takes up the last quarter or so of the movie, pivots on issues of roles and titles. The word "mother" is of practical import for this fight—as noted above, the law at that time overtly favored mothers—but also of almost totemic significance. And while Ted loses in court, his ultimate victory, Joanna's last-minute recognition of his primacy as parent, can also be tied to the success of arguments that are underpinned by an interesting evolution in the language used by the three main actors in the drama, Ted, Joanna, and Margaret.

When Ted initially seeks legal counsel, to defend against Joanna's attempt to wrest custody from him, his attorney is blunt both about his chances and about where the battle will have to focus: "The burden is on us to prove that she's an unfit mother," he says. "In most cases involving a child that young the court tends to side with the mother."

That is to say that Ted, as the father—even as the parent who cared for his son after the child's mother abandoned them (echoes of *Kevin Hill*)—is guilty until proven innocent and that Joanna, by virtue of the badge of motherhood, is innocent until proven guilty (a burden of proof that will be hard for Ted to meet).

By this point in the movie, Ted has become the opposite of what he was in the beginning. He started out in strong support of a traditional, gendered division of labor and primarily concerned about work. The lawyer is telling him that he is now fighting *against* tradition, and Ted's response, when he is warned about the likely high financial cost of such a battle, is that he will "pay anything."

He doesn't care about money now.

This is a complete reversal from Ted's position at the beginning of the movie: As Joanna is trying to get past him, to leave, Ted grouses that he was late getting home because he was out "bringing home the bacon." Clearly, for most of their marriage, that economic and material activity was much more important than anything as "trivial" as taking care of the emotional needs of his family. Hours later, on his first morning as a single father, as he trashes the kitchen in his inept attempts to make breakfast for the two of them, he mutters to Billy that "not only does Daddy have to go out and bring home the bacon, now he has to cook it too."

In her testimony, Joanna repeatedly invokes motherhood as a title rather than an activity. That is, her claim on the child is one of biology and "gender right" rather than one based on what she has done for, or to, her son:

> It was only after therapy [she testifies] I realized that just because I needed another creative outlet than my child, that didn't make me a bad mother.
>
> He's my child. I love him.
>
> I know I left my son. I know that that's a terrible thing to do.
>
> I had to believe it was the best thing for him. I've worked very hard to become a whole human being. I don't think I should be punished for that.
>
> Billy's only seven years old. He needs me. I'm not saying he doesn't need his father. But I really believe he needs me more.
>
> I was his mommy for five and a half years. And Ted took over that role for eighteen months. But I don't know how anybody could believe that I have less of a stake in mothering that little boy than Mr. Kramer does.
>
> I'm his mother. *I'm* his mother [emphasis indicated by inflection in the movie].

She saves her most powerful ammunition for last: Her husband took over being "mommy"; how can he have more of a stake in "mothering"?

She. is. Billy's. Mother.

While these are powerful claims—*How, after all, can he fight on this linguistic terrain? How can he credibly claim to be a better mother?*—the evolution of the language used in the film leads us to the conclusion that Ted actually *is* a good mother. We've seen his behavior change, and we've heard him *called* a mother, and we have nodded in agreement.

More interesting still, she is now essentially taking the position that Ted took in the beginning of the movie. Her claims rest on tradition, on the mother's traditional right to the child, and on her interest in personal development (read: career). But this is *exactly* the position that the movie has spent most of its energy discrediting.

Margaret testifies next, and she attempts, with limited success, to press a claim for fatherhood and to certify the ways in which Ted has changed.

"Mr. Kramer is a very devoted father. . . ." she tells the court. "He's a wonderful father."

After her testimony, still on the stand, over the judge's gavel, she addresses Joanna, tries to say things more clearly than she was able to before:

"Joanna, things are not the same now. Ted is not the same man. You don't know how hard he's tried. They're beautiful together. If you could see them together, maybe you wouldn't be here now."

She starts out here testifying to his qualifications and qualities as a father, an appeal to tradition. But she clearly realizes that those claims are not sufficiently convincing; Ted no longer fits the mold of a traditional father. In her additional, shouted, more direct plea, she goes farther.

Ted is "not the same man," just a few words short of saying what we are being pushed to see in a variety of ways, that he is "not a man." He's "tried hard," a counterweight to the traditional accusation that men don't try hard enough—on emotional terrain generally, with women in relationships, with their children. "They're beautiful together," a much softer evocation of the father-child relationship, implying nurture above mere competence.

Ted's testimony uses a number of tactics, and while these tactics are not successful in legal context, they are the tactics that succeed morally and dramatically and ultimately succeed outside the court; they are the values that we, the audience, are meant to respect and to identify with.

First, he uses the word "parent," which has been little heard in the movie and is almost completely absent from the previous court testimony. Joanna uses the word "mother" as shield and weapon; Margaret attempts to infuse value and new meaning into the word "father." But Ted makes the most egalitarian claim by stressing the word "parent."

Second, he bases his arguments not on symbolism but on acts. He says, in effect, "Judge me not by who or what I am but by what I have done." This echoes other resonant moral calls, such as the one made by Martin Luther King Jr. that we should judge people not by the color of their skins but by the content of their characters.

Finally, unable to play the motherhood card, Ted does the next best thing. He talks about "home," a word that is often gendered as a female word but that allows space for Ted to insert himself more easily than he can fully assume the mantle of "motherhood."

In that sense, he is making an egalitarian appeal, combined with an appeal to necessity. He has done what had to be done. The fact that he has done what had to be done in violation of tradition and, at least to some degree, against self-interest makes his actions that much more creditable, at least in personal terms. At the same time, in legal terms, we know that he is in trouble, bucking an entrenched norm. He begins:

> My ex-wife says that she loves Billy and I believe she does. But I don't think that's the issue here. If I understand it correctly, what means the most here is what's best for our son, what's best for Billy.
>
> My wife used to always say to me, "Why can't a woman have the same ambitions as a man?"
>
> I think you're right (*looking at Joanna*). Maybe I learned that much.

But by the same token, I'd like to know, what law is it that says a woman is a better *parent (emphasizing in inflection)*, simply by virtue of her sex. You know I've had a lot of time to think about what it is that makes someone a good parent.

It has to do with *constancy*, it has to do with patience, it has to do with listening to him, it has to do with *pretending* to listen to him when you can't even listen anymore. It has to do with love, like she was saying. And I don't know where it's written that says that a woman has a corner on that market, that a man has any less of those emotions than a woman does.

Billy has a home with me. I've made it the best I could. It's not perfect; I'm not a perfect parent. Sometimes I don't have enough patience and I forget that he's a kid. But I'm *there.*

I get up in the morning, and we eat breakfast, and he talks to me, and we go to school, and at night we have dinner together, and we talk then, and I read to him, and . . . and we've built a life together. And we love each other.

If you destroy that, it may be irreparable.

Joanna, don't do that, please. Don't do it twice to him.

The cross-examination of Joanna focuses on trying to make her look like a bad woman and a bad mother; the cross-examination of Ted focuses on trying to make him look like a bad man and a bad father.

The attack on his manly credentials is chiefly economic. He lost a job because of time taken off to take care of his son.

"He pretends to fitness," Joanna's lawyer tells the court, as I noted earlier, "when he cannot hold a job."

That is to say, fitness to be a father is tied exclusively to economic power, which echoes a complaint in one of the previously cited letters to the *New York Times*. A mother provides emotional support for a child; a father's role is often relegated to the provision of financial support.

The degree to which this kind of inappropriate gender behavior weakens his position is made clear by an interaction in which the opposing attorney badgers him about missing a deadline because Billy had been sick, with a fever of 104.

Ted eventually shouts back at the attorney in frustration—his child was sick, what could he do!—and the judge admonishes him that if he cannot control his temper, he will be held in contempt.

The irony is manifest: He has become emotional about the well-being of his child, a characteristic that would be taken for granted as appropriate, even laudable, for a woman. In doing so, however, he has lost control—we might even say become shrill—and he is warned that continuing in this vein (arguably both the outburst and his "unnatural" concern for his child) is reason to hold him in contempt. We might hear some double meaning in the word "contempt" in this context, both the legal sense and the personal sense.

When his attorney notifies Ted that they've lost the custody fight, the language he uses is noteworthy.

He says, "The judge went for motherhood right down the line."

But the resonance of the word "home," which ultimately changes Joanna's mind, is also clear. Ted uses it on the witness stand. He also evokes it less directly through linguistic cues evident in the stress that Hoffman puts on certain words in his monologue: Parenting, he says, is about *constancy*; he concedes that he is not a perfect parent, "but I'm *there*."

After he breaks the news to Billy, Billy's response is, "If I don't like it, can I come home?" And, in the movie's final scene, when Joanna capitulates, she says, "I came here to take my son home. And I realize he already *is* home."

The word "father" couldn't quite stretch to fit the new Ted; the word "mother" was repeatedly applied but didn't quite stick; above all, in the end, he is credited with creating a real "home" for his son.

Stealing "Home"?

Not everyone saw *Kramer vs. Kramer* as an indicator of progress.

Film critic Molly Haskell, writing as a guest columnist in the "Hers" column in the *New York Times* in February 1982, for example, was skeptical that the movie really said much about genuine or durable change on the ground, writing in part:

> What distinguishes this latest cycle of noble movie daddies is the implication that they herald a new era: that at last men are reclaiming the emotional and domestic terrain they have so long neglected. So why am I griping? Isn't this precisely what women have been pleading for—a greater sharing of the joys and burdens of the home? I guess I'd be more encouraged if I felt these fables really did represent a deeper and more long-term commitment by men.[35]

Unlike Haskell, I *don't* see the movie as either fable or anomaly. I believe it *did* call attention to a nascent "deeper and long-term commitment," to a change that was in motion and one that has accelerated over time—one documented by the census bureau statistics cited earlier in this chapter.

Elsewhere in the article, Haskell complains, as I cited earlier, "The supreme irony of 'Kramer vs. Kramer' was that here at last was a film that took on the crisis central to the modern woman's life, that is, the three-ring circus of having to hold down a job, bring up a child and manage a house simultaneously, and who gets the role? Dustin Hoffman."

As I have been at pains to acknowledge beginning in my Introduction, I understand her frustration. But indicting the movie for stealing "women's issues" is just another kind of "maternal gatekeeping." Is it more important that we focus on the double yoke of family and work as a women's issue or that we work on solving the problem for everyone?

Bill Clinton did not sign a "maternity leave" act in 1993, for example; he signed the Family and Medical Leave Act (FMLA), referred to earlier in this chapter. That change in nomenclature in no way diminished the good that this legislation has done for women. We need to work on solving issues rather than on arguing over who owns them.

How Do Men Get Home?

The routes that Mr. Banks and Ted Kramer take to greater involvement with their children, to becoming better, more involved fathers, are torturous.

In the world of *Mary Poppins*, a father would have to be crazy to *mother*. Disney takes us right to the brink of the rationality/emotionality split and then pulls us back, toys with the idea of radical change, of a more gender-balanced division of child care, and then gives us a smaller, more incremental and therefore more easily digestible change instead. As I point out in the first section of this chapter, the connection between nurturance and insanity is a road well traveled, a story often told, both in art and in life. George Banks needs a magical push to break out of his repressed conventionality. But magic, in the person of Mary Poppins, is sent packing once the nuclear family has been reconstituted.

Fifteen years later, Ted Kramer asserts a much more enduring claim for a man's emotional connection to home and family. In part, *Kramer vs. Kramer* represents a new twist on an old motif: *Mothering* may not be manly, but shouldering responsibilities as necessity dictates is. The "father (or surrogate father) left caring for the cute tyke" wasn't by any means a radical new image in 1979. In movies and on television, male-headed households—*My Three Sons, Family Affair, The Courtship of Eddie's Father*—had been around for decades.

What *was* different about *Kramer vs. Kramer* is that the focus was not on Ted trying to remarry—so that he could "obtain" another woman to take care of his son. He was not fighting to reconstitute the nuclear family, centered on Husband and Wife; he was fighting to preserve the Parent/Child family.

The transformations of both movie fathers can be seen as epiphanic moments, a literary device borrowed from spiritual and religious experience. These epiphanies are most easily recognizable in Christian art: the saint in a painting or a stained glass window, head tilted back, face illuminated by a beam of light from above—Divine inspiration—a crystallized moment of revelation, a flash of understanding and transformation.

Mr. Banks has such a moment in the midst of being fired: *Things don't have to be this way!*

Ted Kramer has his moment in the hospital emergency room: *I belong with my child!*

We have such moments in our day-to-day lives as well, rare but hard to miss.

Chapter 7, for example, details the story of Ronnie and Eva Huang. The Huangs know the exact point at which they had their epiphanic moment about how they were going to take care of their son Lucius.

Just as grammar didn't keep women out of traditionally male occupations, I don't mean to argue here that media images have kept men out of the domestic sphere. But just as language either encourages us toward or warns us away from any number of possibilities, media images provide us with either positive or negative impressions about who we can be and how we can live.

Clearly, progress has been made from *Mary Poppins* to *Kramer vs. Kramer*, and progress as well over the course of the latter movie. Ted doesn't become closer to his son because he's crazy. At first he does so because he has to.

But by the end of the movie, he is fighting for his son because that's what he *wants*, because of the fierce love he has for his child.

How fatherly.

7

Ronnie Huang: What If We *Don't* Put Him in Day Care?

I figured out real early that it doesn't make a difference what you listen to or what you hear from other people or the doctors or the books or the experts or anything. Because, eventually, you'll find two that contradict. So you have to do what feels right to you.

—RONNIE HUANG

Ronnie Huang[1] can tell you how many degrees hotter you would feel on average wearing black motorcycle leathers compared to white on a sunny summer day. A software consultant who recently changed careers to become a computer science teacher at a prestigious New England prep school, he has an engineer's enthusiasm for specificity, a good memory, and a predilection for odd bits of information about how things work. And—as you might have guessed—he's also a motorcycle enthusiast.

For the three and a half years following the birth of his first son, Lucius, Ronnie was the at-home parent. With the birth of their second son, Benjamin, he and his wife Eva swapped roles: She stayed home and he went back to work. When Benjamin was old enough to go to school, both of his parents resumed full-time jobs and continued to share the work of parenting.

Ronnie's short black hair is just beginning to be flecked with a little white; he is somewhat slightly built but retains the carriage of the track athlete he was in high school, along with an energetic gait. He's quick to laugh, interested in hearing what other people have to say and in learning new things, and just as quick to correct you when you're wrong.

"No," he'll say flatly, shaking his head emphatically and pursing his lips, "that's not true."

It isn't that he's being rude or contrarian; it's just that if he *knows* you're wrong, he's going to tell you.

Facts are facts.

He and his wife were both born in the early 1960s, and both grew up in New York City, Eva in Manhattan, Ronnie mostly in Queens.

The middle child in a family of five, he had an older and a younger brother and an older and a younger sister. His mother was born in the Caribbean, in Jamaica, to Chinese immigrant parents; his father was born in China's Canton Province.

Eva has short black hair, Page Boy cut, glasses, and dark eyes, an almost imperceptible accent. She was born in Hong Kong. When she was ten years old, her eldest sister married an American citizen, and the whole family moved to the United States. She grew up in Chinatown— where Ronnie's family also lived until he was six. She has two sisters, fourteen and sixteen years older, respectively, and a brother three years her junior.

"It was really like having three mothers," she recalls.

In both families, the fathers were restaurant cooks, Eva's in China-town, Ronnie's, for a number of years, at a restaurant in New Jersey— which meant that Ronnie's father was gone six days a week.

In Hong Kong, Eva's mother had been a stay-at-home parent; in the United States, she worked as a seamstress. One of the dominant themes of Eva's childhood was the fact that her parents were almost always working.

"That's really typical of Chinese immigrant families," she says. "You don't really see your parents that much."

The division of labor in Ronnie's childhood home was traditional, he says. His mother did all the usual domestic work; as the children got older, she delegated some of the work to them.

Ronnie's parents did a lot of arguing when he was growing up, though he can't seem to remember much of what they were arguing about. His parents separated when he was ten years old and subsequently divorced. He and the other children stayed with their mother, who eventually remarried.

In part due to the domestic tumult of his childhood, before even beginning to contemplate what his married life would be like, he says, "First I had to leap over the fact that, *yes, one day, I'm going to get married*."

That didn't start out a foregone conclusion for him.

What he remembers thinking, through high school, into college and beyond, was "Why would anyone *want* to get married? Why would anyone *want* to have kids?"

Television offered no useful perspective, no viable alternative models. Watching *The Brady Bunch* or *The Partridge Family*, he thought: "No, that doesn't look anything like our family at all!"

Ronnie and Eva met and began dating as undergraduates at Cornell.

After they graduated, when they were living together, and then when they were married, Ronnie says they began to get a broader view of family life, some of this through exposure to the family lives of older colleagues who already had children.

"You visit their homes," he says. "You see their families. I don't know if they argue all the time, but they don't do it in front of you."

Why Am I Giving My Three-Month-Old Over to Somebody Else?

In 1995, when their son Lucius was born, Ronnie and Eva were both doing well, working as software engineers in the high-tech corridor outside Boston. They had been bringing in two incomes for ten years; they'd owned their own home for six of those ten years.

"At that time," Ronnie says, "we didn't have any car payments and we didn't have any student loans. We had already paid those off."

Day-care slots at good facilities—then, as always—were tight. And they had started both searching and researching during Eva's pregnancy. They had decided where they wanted to send Lucius and had been wait-listed. A space opened up about four weeks before they were ready, and they put down a deposit.

And then—the day before Lucius was to start day care—his parents thought: *Why?*

Why should they have a child and then almost immediately shunt him off into the care of other people?

If they *didn't* want to do that, what were their other options?

First and foremost: Would they still be able to pay the mortgage if one of them stopped bringing in an income?

"Eva and I said, 'There's just no way we can send him off to day care,'" Ronnie remembers about that day. "It didn't seem like the right thing to do. I don't know if *emotionally* is the right word—or a combination of *emotionally* and *intellectually*. It seemed like, when you have a three-month-old, it's like *Why am I giving my three-month-old over to somebody else to take care of?*"

His voice has a rising inflection as he says this last part; he tilts his head to the side and knits his eyebrows in emphasizing their perplexity—newly discovered but intense—over this question.

"It didn't make any sense to Eva," he says. "It didn't make any sense to me."

But then he goes back and considers this again, puzzling over the question, rethinking it. "It had to be emotional," he says finally. "Because, intellectually, it *does* make sense."

"I don't know if this is one of the places where you'd say that the *Eureka! Phenomenon* did it," he continues, "I just thought *I'll quit my job.* Intuitively, it was something like *Oh, I want to do this.* I didn't get any disagreement from Eva, and I did get support, so it just seemed like the right thing to do."

The *Eureka! Phenomenon,* of course, ties in with previous sections of this book—with Chapter 6, on movies, at the top of the list. It's an epiphanic moment.

In *Mary Poppins*, George Banks realizes, in the midst of something akin to a psychotic episode, that his job is not that significant a loss, that his family is more important. In *Kramer vs. Kramer,* Ted, his son bleeding and crying on an emergency room stretcher a few feet away from him, realizes in a flash of hot anger that he's not going to let *anything* come between him and his child.

Ronnie Huang came to a similar pair of conclusions.

And if he can't really say whether he was likely moving incrementally in the direction of those ideas, of those feelings, of that decision, for some time—weeks or months or years—the actual decision point is crystal clear:

Are we putting our son in day care tomorrow?

No.

As in other families we've looked at, financial circumstances played a role in the decision; they weighed the trade-offs; they did the math. As is true for many Americans faced with career or family decisions, insurance weighed in their calculations as well. Doing contract work, Ronnie was making more money at that point, but Eva's job provided their medical coverage.

Back to work Eva went.

Ronnie began figuring out how to be a stay-at-home dad. And out the window went the day-care deposit.

Who Does What?

"In general," Ronnie says, "Eva and I are interchangeable."

By this he means there is little or nothing that either of them can't or won't do regarding kid care.

But he then points to a couple of interesting exceptions.

"Lucius considers me the primary caretaker," he says, and "Benjamin considers Eva the primary caretaker."

In other words, the children are slightly more bonded to and identified with the parent they spent the most time with during infancy and during their preschool years.

Makes sense.

Rather than the "maternal bond" that many people see as a matter of wiring, Lucius and Benjamin demonstrate a "parental bond," a kind of gender-neutral imprinting, a product of their personal experiences.[2]

The other point Ronnie makes, naturally enough, is "We have different interests. For example, Eva doesn't like [bicycle] riding. When I take care of [the kids], I take them bike riding."

Lucius Huang's short, glossy, black hair usually looks recently cut, the edges clean and blunt. He has brown eyes, glasses, a quick smile, and a soft laugh. At eleven, he's both physically and intellectually energetic, serious when focused but often playful as well.

His younger brother, Benjamin, is more reticent, a somewhat shy eight-year-old.

Looking to his own future, considering who might do what when he has children, Lucius seems to have the same functionalist attitude that his parents have had throughout his childhood.

"I don't see anything that would make a *difference*," he says, about the question of how domestic duties would be divided. His inflection rises slightly as he responds, his emphasis not mocking the question but embedding a gentle, slightly quizzical counterquestion of his own in the answer.

"If it gets done, it gets done," he tells me, stressing the importance of concrete results over role.

"If it doesn't, it doesn't," he adds, reinforcing the point that the more relevant question is not "who" but "whether," not how the labor is divided but the end result.

When asked about how his parents divide things up at home, Lucius mostly just shrugs. His response to every category is "Sometimes my mom, sometimes my dad."

The week that we spoke, the family was gearing up to move—for his father's new teaching job. Eva, who was still doing software work but had moved into management, was particularly busy in the office, Ronnie particularly busy at home.

As in other households, Ronnie and Eva don't do everything in exactly the same way, and this extends to how they deal with their children. Sometimes the differences are purely matters of style or habit.

When they first swapped roles and Eva became the at-home parent, for example, Lucius would point out how the way she did things differed from the way Ronnie did things: When he cut sandwiches in half, he made them into triangles, while Eva made them into rectangles; when she made toast, she used the toaster, while he used a pan; when he brought the children back from an outing, he would always say, "Home sweet home" as they pulled into the garage.

In the matter of style, Ronnie says, "clothes are probably not a good example. As you've probably noticed," he laughs, "neither Eva nor I are very fashionable."

But in that area, as in a few others, they have somewhat different functional concerns on occasion. Recall that black motorcycle leathers can make you feel significantly hotter (by as much as five degrees). Ronnie applies this knowledge when dressing the kids on warm days; he's a bit more careful than Eva is in avoiding dark colors.

Boundaries and Intellect

Eva explains her flexibility in approaching family structure—who does what and how things get done—as having come in part from the impact that immigrating to the United States as a child had on her. She'd had some preconceived notions about America before coming here, largely gleaned from television and movies, but the reality she encountered, she said, "was nothing like that. It wasn't like houses with white picket fences."

"If you think about someone leaving their country, going somewhere else, when they're ten," she says, it's an experience that fundamentally alters how you see life, how you see possibilities.

The rules of the country you were born in don't apply anymore, she explains, but it can also be difficult to feel fully integrated into the country you've moved to.

"There's no boundaries," she says. "Because so much change has gone on in my life, everything's adaptable. Being adaptive is really what I gained out of all this."

In a sense—both while she was growing up and then on into adulthood—her vision of how things *could* or *should* be in any number of areas in her life was a blank canvas.

As she notes, this is a useful characteristic, both in the professional sphere and in the personal sphere. Cultural dislocation can be difficult, but it can also be liberating.

Eva might be said to have an attitude toward a great number of things that can be embodied in the almost reflexive question *Why not?* Ronnie's attitude, by way of comparison, can be compressed into the only slightly shorter, and somewhat vehement, *Why?* He is open to all kinds of questions, answers, and solutions, but you have to convince him.

Ronnie seems to have adopted this attitude fairly early on in his life, a critical and analytical stance toward a great deal of what was presented to him as fact, tradition, or requirement, resisting and then rejecting external standards of "how things are supposed to be," far more concerned with doing things in a way that made sense to him.

"I *still* do that!" he said exuberantly in a subsequent conversation.

This approach made for a somewhat bumpy childhood but probably made him a more successful adult. Independence is a quality that we often laud in theory but punish in practice. Children in particular can be whipsawed by this inconsistency—*Yes, yes, I want you to be an independent thinker, but right now, just be quiet and do what I'm telling you to do!* We are more likely to reap the benefits of this approach in adulthood. In terms of his relationship with his mother in particular, he describes himself as the child who gave her the most trouble when he was growing up but who is now the closest to her of her five children.

He describes as well a mutual respect that has grown between them since he left for college. Perhaps, he says, because she was raised in the Caribbean, she is somewhat less tradition bound than Ronnie's father; she's come to appreciate and support the things that he does and the ways that he does them, both in his personal life and in his professional life. When he learned to ride a motorcycle, she thought that was great; her reaction was the same when he entered graduate school with an eye toward becoming a teacher.

He looks back fondly on some aspects of his childhood.

"There are certain Jamaican foods," he says, for example, "that my mom used to make when I was growing up and I've asked her for the recipes to see if I can make them."

Food is also one link to Chinese culture that he would like to hand on to his own children.

"I like the way, during the holidays, all of the family gets together," he says. "Eva's parents have a bunch of traditional foods that her mom knows how to make for those particular occasions. And one of the things that I wanted to do was to see if I could learn how to make those things, so that we could carry them on to our kids. So on such and such a day you would know that the family is getting together to make those foods."

Though his father cooked professionally, Ronnie doesn't talk about learning recipes from him—of course for many restaurant cooks, the *last* thing they want to do when they come home from work is involve themselves once again in food preparation.

"My dad immigrated directly from China," Ronnie says, and "there the division [between what men do and what women do] is even more strict than in the United States. The only thing that has value in the Chinese tradition is the sons."

"Even in the hierarchy of the males," he adds, "it's the oldest male [the first son] who has the stature in the family," whose responsibilities are second only to those of the father.

As a child, Ronnie resented this, not because he was the middle child but because, as someone with a strong, independent spirit, he disliked the supervisory interference of his older brother. He has consciously and vehemently avoided that sibling hierarchy with his own children.

"In ten years," he says, "I've never said to Lucius, *You're the older brother; you have to take care of your younger brother.* It will never come out of my mouth, from now until I die."

Between *Why?* and *Why not?* then, both Eva and Ronnie are people who don't tend to feel restrained by precedent or by restrictions that don't make sense to them: Eva's childhood experiences knocked down boundaries for her; Ronnie's instinct seems almost always to have been to question boundaries and then knock them down on his own.

Arguably, the fact that both Ronnie and Eva are computer scientists by training has also played a role in how they approach all kinds of questions and decisions. They incline toward functional results and creative approaches; they are less concerned about, interested in, or bound by orthodoxy.

One way to think of a piece of software is as a giant flowchart—or perhaps, more accurately, a nested and overlapping series of flowcharts that form a larger whole. On the one hand, designing something like that, or one of its subunits, requires a logical approach and a clear field of vision, the ability to project multiple possibilities and their likely consequences, to handle large numbers of variables and permutations.

Programming is about logic, about numbers, about mathematics.

On the other hand, mathematics has been linked with music for good reasons that go back centuries and across cultures. Mathematics cannot be reduced to arithmetic, the tedious and mechanistic pushing around of numbers. Mathematical problems and solutions have a flow to them: Some problems can be solved solely via logic—or using "brute force," either human or electronic—but the most complex problems require creative approaches.

To work in computer science, in either software or hardware, requires logic, rigor, and clear thinking, but it also requires flexibility, an intellectual approach both subtle and supple. Both sides of that ledger of skills are useful in approaching how we decide on domestic divisions of labor and how we interact with children.

"Some problems in computer science and engineering are [Eureka-based]," Ronnie says. "A lot of them are still iterative: You have a set of requirements and you have to fulfill those requirements. You can do it a piece at a time; you get it done over time."

Ronnie describes both himself and Eva as intelligent and respectful of each other. He doesn't make decisions for her; she doesn't make decisions for him; they tend toward mutually agreed-on experimentation.

They discuss issues and then, he says, it's "Well, let's see what happens if we go this way."

What about *Masculine* Intuition?

All of Ronnie's emphasis on intellect, research, and rational decision making notwithstanding, he is the first to admit that parenting pushes one—has pushed him—to develop and to rely more on intuitive judgments.

That shift is clear in the epiphanic moment he had over deciding not to send Lucius to day care.

"It didn't make sense" to put him in day care, he said at first.

But then he went back, rethought the matter, and amended what he'd said.

It *did* make sense.

But it didn't *feel* right.

And while he went into fatherhood reading about child development issues, analyzing his son's needs, collecting information in a variety of ways, it became clear to him early on, he says, that there are limits to how much you can learn, intellectually, about caring for a child.

After all, he points out, you can find a book, an expert, a Web site for whatever approach you want to take: One year babies are supposed to sleep on their stomachs, the next on their sides, the year after that on their backs. And you are constantly assured that *this time* the information is definitive and that you ignore it at your peril.

"It doesn't make a difference what you listen to or what you hear from other people or the doctors or the books or the experts or anything," he says. "Because, eventually, you'll find two that contradict. So you have to do what feels right to you."

"Now, we're relying more and more on intuition," he says of the changes that parenthood has introduced to his household. "And that's kind of new to me."

If some of Tom Andrejev's experiences, detailed in Chapter 3, point up how hard men have to work to demonstrate that we are not dangerous—to children, to women, to laundry, to small animals—the question of intuition highlights a more subtle problem, just as pervasive and perhaps just as intense: Do men have the *emotional* skills needed to take care of children, to notice what needs to be noticed, to take the appropriate tone and approach?

Consider that it is surely a minority of women who worry that the fathers of their children might constitute a physical threat to their own children. Many more—*not* a majority, I would hope, but it would be hard to measure such a thing—harbor serious concerns about whether or not these same men possess the skills, either learned or intuitive, to care for their children "properly."

Properly is a loaded word, as in:

"My child is excitable" versus "Your child doesn't know how to behave properly."

"I've dressed my son creatively" versus "You don't seem to know how to dress a child properly."

"My daughter is an enthusiastic eater" versus "Your daughter doesn't know how to eat properly."

Whether as a matter of logic or a matter of intuition, we often disagree about what constitutes proper child care, proper parenting, or proper behavior—for "children of all ages." That's true of Americans as a society; it's also true within many individual families.

These disagreements, moreover, frequently fall along gender lines. And even people with strongly rooted egalitarian convictions often come to see this as a matter of "gender wiring."

Recall Andrea John-Smith's impressions, from Chapter 5. A baby's cry, she said, hers or anyone else's, simply cut through her in her daughter's first few years; she found it almost physically painful, impossible to ignore, and ascribed this reaction essentially to biology and to gender. She didn't think all women have this response, but she didn't know *any* men who did. And while she knew *some* men who had "taught" themselves to respond to children the way she feels they need to be responded to—her husband Darryl included—learned response is clearly second-best to intuitive response.

The question of intuition, then, is a serious one, and not just as it relates to the Huangs. If we believe that intuition is key to parenting, that the degree to which people are in touch with their feelings is a benchmark of their ability to parent, then how—or the degree to which—we "gender" intuition either lets men in or keeps them out.

Mostly, it keeps us out.

It shouldn't.

In Chapter 8—in the context of analyzing images in television commercials—I briefly go back to the issue of language and look at a couple of word sets: Soccer Mom, Soccer Dad, Soccer Parent; Working Mother, Working Father, Working Parent.

Try this, as a warm-up for those comparatives: *Masculine Intuition.*

Does that have a slightly contradictory, slightly dissonant ring to it?

You would not be alone in having that reaction. A Google search for the terms "Masculine Intuition" and "Feminine Intuition" yields almost twenty times more hits for the latter phrase over the former (see Appendix A).[3]

This reflects a deep conviction, across a broad swath of cultures and a long sweep of time: Women *feel*. And feeling, of course, as Ronnie has observed and, as any good parent will tell you, is key to child care.

We can argue about what it is that men do, by way of contrast: Think? Act? Hit people?

And so we come back to the question of nature versus nurture.

In 1992, in the introduction to a collection of essays he edited, *Men, Masculinity, and the Media,* Steve Craig wrote that men's studies shared with feminist theory the key concept that "most (if not all) behavior commonly associated with gender is seen as learned rather than innate, and biological theories that see gender differences as 'natural' are themselves considered to be the product of these cultural distinctions" (parenthetical phrase in original text).[4]

That's not a very nuanced statement. The tagging of all studies of innate gender differences as culturally solipsistic—a way of saying, "You may *think* you are coming to empirical conclusions, but *really* you've just been acculturated into a belief system"—even takes a step in the direction of "data proofing" the argument.

I am keenly aware of the danger of essentialism, of the horrific purposes to which it can be bent: "We know that Group B has characteristic Y; it is therefore perfectly reasonable to discriminate against them, to limit the opportunities they have, or to kill all of them." That's not hyperbole; into the twenty-first century, in some places, it is government policy.

In looking at and attempting to analyze language, images, and narratives, I *agree* with a large part of what Craig is saying; in significant ways, gender is a cultural construct; I believe in both the utility and the reality of role plasticity. It would be more convenient for me if I completely accepted Craig's position.

I'll risk enraging the Nurture contingent, however, by suggesting that hormones matter.

Crudely put: If you have a higher level of estrogen, you're more likely to hug people; if you have a higher level of testosterone, you're more likely to hit people.

But we are not simply walking conglomerations of glands. And I don't think that endocrinology is either destiny or conspiracy. More interesting, and more directly relevant to both Ronnie's experience and to the experience of fathers in general, estrogen is not exclusively female nor testosterone exclusively male, and the balance between these hormones in our bodies fluctuates drastically over time. Pregnancy, childbirth, and the introduction of a baby into a household, moreover, induce hormonal changes *in men*[5] as well as in women.

I can't say why Ronnie Huang chose to go in the direction he went, the night before his son was to be sent to day care. *Ronnie* can't really say. We make decisions for rational reasons, we calculate costs and benefits, but we also, perhaps most often, end up doing what *feels* right.

It didn't *feel* right to give his son over to institutional care that early.

Whatever else sparked that feeling, Ronnie may also have been chemically nudged in that direction. A variety of studies have shown that men experience significant hormonal changes, both before the birth of their children and during the first few months of their children's lives:[6] a decrease in testosterone, an increase in estrogen, and increases in prolactin—the hormone that promotes lactation in women—and in cortisol, a stress hormone that, in women, has been correlated with emotional bonding to a newborn.

Does this mean that women are "naturally" better parents, because their physical and chemical responses to children are stronger?

Not necessarily.

It provides, however, another useful potential puzzle piece, more data to sketch and to fill out the context of parenting and childrearing.

I don't want to see women boxed into child care any more than I want to see men boxed out. I'm not an essentialist, and I'm well aware of the dangers that lurk in that direction.

The lesson?

We should reject *bad science*, not science as a whole.

Throw out the bath water; keep the baby.

Ronnie Huang thought about what he wanted to do for his son, about what kind of childhood he wanted him to have, about the financial and professional consequences. And then he did what felt right.

Sounds like a *natural* parent to me.

8

. . . .

TV Commercials and the
New American Family

. . . .

Kix Cereal: Kid-Tested, Mother-Approved

*Not sure which Robitussin is right for your cold? Ask
Dr. Mom.*

Most of us still go out to see at least *some* movies. Other movies—along with video of varying types—we bring *to* us, via purchase or rental, in the mail, on the Web, through whatever counts as TV from house to house and year to year.

Advertising is fundamentally different, an increasingly pervasive multimedia *swarm* with a growing degree of intelligence and intentionality. From logos to product placement, from spam to Webverts, we are inundated with ads. There has been a movement afoot for several years now to make ads sufficiently interesting that we will actively seek them out—for entertainment, rather than information—but for the most part we are willing to spend time, money, and effort *not* to see ads (we download, purchase, and tinker with blocking software of varying kinds; we fast-forward through; we edit out).

The ads find us anyway.

Having already looked at television and at movies, in this chapter I'll look at some of the ways advertising shapes how we see ourselves, our culture, and our possibilities—and at what some ads suggest about the status and the characteristics of fathers.

Geertz's famous definition of culture, one last time, is "the set of stories we tell ourselves about ourselves." And ads, I would argue, are the most compact and—in modern context—the most prolific genre of stories to which we are exposed.

Our definitions of what constitute legitimate areas of study have expanded in recent decades; analyzing television and movies isn't looked down on quite as much, or looked at with the same degree of skepticism. The analysis of advertising, however, is still a bit of a hard sell.

For many scholars, this kind of analysis has too much of the taint of commerce attached to it. And for the average person—for the average student—the response is often "They're *just* ads. They don't mean much of anything beyond *Pay attention* or *Buy this*."

This latter response usually has less to do with whether or not people see ads as a "legitimate" area of study and more to do with the question of how much useful information they can give us about ourselves.

A great deal of information, I would argue, in a very small space.

We are exposed to advertising on a daily basis, and the sheer volume of our exposure is impressive—or frightening, depending on how you look at it. Feminist advertising critic Jean Kilbourne, for example, estimates that the average American is exposed to something in the neighborhood of three thousand advertisements per day.[1]

If that number seems preposterously high—wherever you are—look around and start counting.

You aren't just looking (or listening) for television or radio commercials or scanning for text or graphic advertisements. Look for labels, for logos, for objects so familiar you've stopped seeing them. Think about how many cans or bottles of soda you see on the average day, for example, each emblazoned with multiple icons or trademark phrases.

Without moving my head, simply looking at my computer, the screen, and the connected peripherals, I can see more than two dozen brand names, logos, icons, or registered trademarks.

As a matter of frequency, of density, of volume, whether we like it or not, ads are everywhere around us, embedded in our environment.

Icons and logos aside, they are most prolific in the cultural products we consume: the movies and videos we watch, the newspapers, magazines, and Web pages we read.

We can't read or watch the stories that entertain or inform us without also reading and watching a whole connected package of ads, which are themselves little stories. Arguably, as much as or even more than the programming they support, these ads *are* the stories of our culture.

How many lines of Hawthorne—or Hemingway or Baldwin—can the average American quote from memory?

And how many fast food chain slogans can the average American quote from memory?

The prosecution rests.

There is also the ever-present matter of money.

TV commercials are dense narratives—usually only thirty seconds long—in which *everything* has to matter, *everything* has to have a purpose, in which no image or action or sound can be wasted. American businesses spend billions of dollars every year on advertising, and this discipline is enforced by the iron laws of commerce and economics, by the money spent on advertising and the money that businesses of various stripes rely on it to bring in. Advertisements have a financial impact because they have a cultural impact. Money spent on ads comes back in the form of profits, or companies go out of business.

I wish there *weren't* so much advertising and I wish it *didn't* impact us.

But it's everywhere. And it does have an impact.

Honey, Is It Okay If I Dry Off the Children in the Microwave?

Dating back to my childhood, the images of men in commercials that I have found most grating—chiefly but not exclusively on television—have been the images of incompetence. I was always irritated by the endless stream of men—some fathers, some not—consistently shown to be incapable of effectively completing pretty much *any* domestic task.

It still makes me sick. Ask Dr. Mom.

On the evidence presented over a period of decades, you would pretty much have to conclude that men are simply handed off from mothers to wives: Clearly, we can't feed or clothe ourselves without constant supervision and assistance. Perish the thought that responsibility for another human being would be entrusted to our care, certainly not any being as precious and vulnerable as a child.

Some people have taken to calling this slapstick figure, prevalent both in sitcoms and in all manner of ads, the *Doofus Dad*. A quick look at a TV commercial for the 2002 Honda Accord shows that he is alive and well into the twenty-first century.

A man in his mid-twenties exits his house and approaches the new Accord in his driveway, a baby in his arms.

"We're gonna do some errands for Momma today," he says singsong to the baby, then notices that a few water drops from the lawn sprinkler have spattered the car. He's clearly upset about this, and then inspiration strikes. Looking around quickly for witnesses, he begins bouncing the baby up and down and back and forth in the air over the car—babytalking as he does: "We're gonna-go-fer-a-ride!"

Then, as part of the baby-bouncing motion, he uses the baby's diaper-clad bottom to wipe off the water drops, nods and smiles in satisfaction, and puts the baby in the back seat, and the commercial ends with the tag line: "The 2002 Honda Accord: You can't explain it until you have one of your own."

Cute: Men don't just baby their cars; for us, our cars *are* our babies.

This kind of humor is effective because some percentage of both men and women can nod their heads in recognition at what they see as an only slightly exaggerated image. We "know" that babies are best cared for by women. Reinforcing that idea is reassuring to women who believe they are more caring and careful with children and to the men who don't really *want* to take responsibility for kids.

Harmless?

Maybe.

It reads a little differently if you're a woman who *wants* her husband to take some or all of the responsibility for child care or if you are a father who takes caring for his children seriously.

Imagine the same commercial, with a mother—instead of a father—cleverly using her child as a car-cleaning rag.

Harmless?

Maybe.

"All in good fun?"

Not really.

A woman performing the same actions would have her character—if not her sanity—called into question; you mess with motherhood at your own peril.

The commercial is chock-a-block with additional details that tell us what men are like with babies, and I'll hit just a few of them quickly.

The baby is being put into the car in a shirt and diaper: no pants, no socks, no shoes. The father isn't carrying a diaper bag: no diapers, no wipes, no bottle—*that's* going to be a fun trip for everybody and soon. Finally, disposable diapers tend to have the absorbent layer on the inside and an impermeable cover on the outside; we have reason to wonder whether or not "whoever diapered the child" put the diaper on inside-out.

What Does It Feel Like to Be a Modern Father?

The durability of the Sadly Bad Dad image on television notwithstanding—he's a nice guy and well intentioned, but don't let him near cooking, cleaning, or children, or *hilarious* chaos will ensue!—the commercial I examine most closely in this chapter is *not* primarily a representation of male incompetence. Rather, this commercial, along with the series of commercials from which it comes, makes important and interesting statements about the *plight* of fathers—and by extension the plight of families—in early twenty-first-century America.

"Business Trip" is a thirty-second television commercial, one of a series of three produced for AT&T Wireless by the advertising firm Goodby, Silverstein & Partners in 2003 as part of the "Reach Out" ad campaign.[2] The three commercials are linked by a recurring theme:

the ability of the cell phone to connect and reconcile family members separated by physical distance.

A close analysis of this commercial, cut by cut, provides an interesting lens through which we can examine contemporary American attitudes toward family, in particular what has changed—and what has *not* changed—regarding gender roles, division of labor, and issues of child care; the commercial also eloquently speaks to the fundamental conflict many of us feel between our obligations to work and our obligations to family.

Just as the issue of redemption formed an important ongoing subtext to the TV series *Kevin Hill* and to the story of the Smith family, some surprising theological resonances lurk—and not too far from the surface—in the background of this commercial as well.

Daddy's *Not* Home

"Business Trip" represents a contemporary counterpoint to the stereotype of the paternal figure whose relationship to nurturance and domesticity is either cold and distant or warm and incompetent. In my view, the commercial speaks to the question of who we want fathers to *be* in the twenty-first century, not always returning easy or happy answers but approaching the contemporary father with a degree of sympathy and respect.

I'll start with a compressed description of the commercial (a full, shot-by-shot description can be found in Appendix B).

A man in a business suit—rumpled, slightly overweight, in early middle age and burdened with luggage—unsuccessfully attempts to insert a keycard into a hotel room door lock; he kneels in front of the door, struggling with the lock. When he gets the door open, we see the room from his point of view: a bed with twin pillows, twin light fixtures attached to the wall above the head of the bed, gray blanket and walls.

We cut to a shot of our businessman sitting on the edge of the mattress, at the foot of the bed, in shirt, boxer shorts, and socks. On his knees is a tray; on the tray is a large white plate, in the middle of which, dwarfed by everything around it, is some item of food—

presumably a piece of meat—roughly the size of a deck of cards and elaborately garnished. The businessman looks something between unimpressed and bewildered by this.

Behind him, and to the right, one corner of the room is a glass cubicle, reflecting the bed, doubling the effect of the twin pillows and lights. Through the glass, we can make out a toilet, a tiled "tray" on the floor and, on the wall above this tray, the edge of something metallic—presumably a shower faucet. We see curtains, gathered in the corners of the cubicle but not pulled closed. All of these features, along with the gray color scheme, make the room look like an elegant prison cell.

We then see him asleep on his back: arms straight out from his body, in scarecrow position. We see this from above, the businessman's head pointed toward the bottom right of the shot, his legs toward the top left.

A yellow taxi moves through a tunnel, away from the light at the entrance. Through the window, we see the businessman's upper body, his head tilted back slightly as he looks upward with an exhausted, forlorn expression on his face.

At the airport, he stands at a security checkpoint, again in scarecrow position, as two people examine him, one with a metal-detecting wand; then we see him running through a crowd, suitcase in one hand, garment bag in the other, newspaper under his arm.

His flight has been delayed and he sits alone in a gate waiting area, looking at his watch. Then we hear a breathy little girl's voice say, "Hi, Daddy."

He turns toward the camera, his face lighting up and softening.

He smiles and says, "Hey, Sweetheart!"

We cut to the face of a little girl, perhaps six or seven years old, curly blonde hair, blue eyes, her face tilted to the left, her cheek resting on her fist.

"I miss you," the father says.

"I miss you, too," she responds.

The camera pulls back and we see father and daughter together. She's sitting on the chair immediately adjacent to his, wearing a red and blue soccer uniform, high socks over shin guards.

"What did you do today?" he asks.

"I played soccer," she says.

As she says her line, other passengers materialize and begin to walk quickly back and forth between the scene we have been watching and the camera. The daughter dematerializes and we see instead only the father, sitting, smiling broadly, animated and talking into a cell phone.

"For your most important calls," an announcer tells us, "Reach Out, on the wireless service America trusts: AT&T Wireless."

The camera pulls back as the businessman continues to talk, though we do not hear his words. The row of chairs he is sitting on is on the airport's second tier; people move along that row from left to right, and vice versa. On the tier below, they move along a corridor from the top of the shot to the bottom, and vice versa. He sits just above and to the right of the intersection of those two lines. The camera moves up, from the second tier to the vaulted skylights above, and the screen fades to white, on which is imposed the AT&T Wireless logo, 800 number, and Web address.

What do we see, hear, imagine, and conclude from this?

I would suggest that three narrative strands are intertwined here and are mutually reinforcing: the core narrative, an interesting subtextual narrative—buried but not too deeply if you know where to dig—and what we might think of as a "supertextual" narrative on top of the main message.

Lots of Ways to Save—or to *Be* Saved—by Using Your Cell Phone

Every commercial has the same core narrative: *Buy our product.*

Often, this is formulated as "You have a problem, and our product is the solution to this problem," which is a way to say, "You're not doing *us* a favor by buying our product; we're doing *you* a favor by offering it to you."

In this case, we can express the problem—in clinical terms—as "insufficient connection between family members."

The solution to the problem of families being separated, of course, is "Get our cell phone service."

In *Mary Poppins*, magic was magic, and it was wielded to heal and bring together the Banks family.

Here the phone is magic—technology is the new *deus ex machina*.

The cell phone is a bridging device, magically transporting family members into each other's work lives to allow them to address—and solve, at least for the moment—problems caused by their separation. This theme is consistent, running through all three commercials in the series.

In one of the other commercials, we see a feuding married couple who reconcile via cell phone instant messaging. In the third, we see an African American woman who listens to a child's piano recital via cell phone while she's on a bus stuck in traffic—some resonance there with Rosa Parks.

That last commercial also deploys an interesting and useful "lack of specificity" regarding family. We might assume the woman and child are mother and son, but we can't be certain; in the recital hall, the cell phone that is transmitting the concert is held by a man whose relationship to the other two characters is also uncertain—*probably* the husband and father, but we don't know that either. We never see his left hand, for example, and so have no opportunity to see if he has a wedding ring on or not—in fact, in one shot, the camera cuts away just as we are about to see his left hand.

What we might call the supertextual narrative—the nice icing on top of the core of pure commerce—in both the concert commercial and in "Business Trip" is very appealing, certainly to me: It is heartbreaking for a parent to be separated from a child; it is a desolating experience.

Here we see this illustrated vividly. The father is miserable until he connects with his daughter, at which point he absolutely lights up. And I think it positive that we are beginning to get representations like this that show men demonstrating emotional connection to their children: love, pain, concern, intensity.

If we look a little more closely, we may also see some interesting linguistic implications here, just beneath the surface, even though the commercial includes only minimal dialogue.

What do we *call* this man, after all? How do we *identify* him? How do we think he identifies himself?

Well, what do we hear and what do we see?

The only name we hear him called is "Daddy."

And everything that he does in the twenty-plus seconds preceding this dialogue is business related; he has no leisure, indeed no *pleasure*, in anything he does—including, perhaps especially, such actions as sleeping and eating, which are supposed to give us some measure of respite. The ad agency, after all, entitled the commercial "Business Trip."

It is reasonable to conclude that what we are seeing is a "Working Father."

And what is his conversation with his daughter focused on? What is she wearing?

They discuss her soccer game; she wears a soccer uniform.

It may be a bit of a leap, but I would on that basis call him, metaphorically at least, a "Soccer Dad."

He's not a "Soccer Dad" on the sidelines—at least not this week— rather he is a Dad connected to his daughter's chosen sport via the umbilicus of his cell phone.

Working Father.

Soccer Dad.

We don't use these phrases much—if at all.

Appendix C contains the results of series of Google searches to back up this contention, a fast and crude method of cultural temperature taking.

In 2004, "working mother" constituted 82 percent of the hits, compared to 3 percent for "working father." "Soccer mom" got 94 percent of the hits, compared to 2 percent for "soccer dad." In 2006, by way of comparison, "working mother" constituted 83 percent of the hits, compared to 4 percent for "working father," with the gender-neutral "working parent" losing a percentage point to both. "Soccer mom," meanwhile, fell to 78 percent of the hits, while "soccer dad" increased to 21 percent.[3]

As I said, we don't use those phrases much, although we are beginning to use them more.

Why?

Our language reflects that we take it for granted that fathers work (outside the home) and that mothers care for children (inside the home). It is the deviation from the perceived norm that encourages us to notice and to name.

A *working* father?

Well (of course!), men work outside the home, whatever else they do. No sense in even pointing this out; it is a statement of the obvious.

A working *mother?*

Mothers are *supposed* to be primarily taking care of their children. We started using the phrase because the deviation from the norm was noteworthy—it's ironic that we still use it now that what it describes is so common.

These cultural generalizations have some statistical basis, obviously. But the numbers are getting stale, and what we are talking about—and *how* we are talking about it—hasn't been keeping pace with either workforce or domestic reality.

So, again, what do we see in this commercial?

We see a "working father" giving emotional attention to his daughter, clearly as much for his own benefit as for hers.

The catch is, he's *phoning it in*—literally.

I'll return to the core narrative here. What any commercial does is give the viewer a very simple proposition: "You have a problem. Our product is the solution."

But really, you have, and the commercial depicts, *two* problems—or, more accurately, competing imperatives—taking care of family and taking care of business.

AT&T Wireless, however—reasonably enough as the spinoff of a venerable and conservative American corporation—is not in the business of social revolution.

So they acknowledge here the conflict at the core of a lot of our lives—point out that being a working father can be as agonizing as being a working mother—but offer *not* to help us change almost unbearably difficult circumstances, but rather to better accommodate to them.

We know you ache. You're a sensitive guy. We feel your pain.

"$39.99 per month to your wireless company and you're clean."

Evenings and weekends free.

Absolution on the cheap.

Kevin Hill spent twenty-two episodes seeking to redeem himself. Clearly he should have just purchased a good phone plan: Our working father takes only thirty seconds to zoom through a subtextual narrative thread, which intertwines a series of visual images, which are stunning in the intensity of their Christian resonance.

Almost the first view that we get of our business traveler is of him on his knees, genuflecting on a red carpet before the door to his hotel room. He gets into the room, eats a lonely (last?) supper, and falls asleep on the bed in a position of crucifixion—which we view from above.

He takes a cab to the airport, looking skyward out the rear window, as if seeking divine solace. At the security checkpoint, he once more assumes the position of crucifixion. Then we again see him from above, one ant among many, as he runs across the concourse.

In the end, he finds salvation and redemption through love, through the purity of his child and of his connection to her. We get an age- and gender-reversed Pietà in the airport: Instead of Mary holding a dead and mutilated Jesus, we have the daughter comforting by her presence—and visibly revivifying—her wounded father.

Then the camera tracks up, from our businessman situated, "on the cross," just above and to the right of two intersecting lines of pedestrian traffic, to the skylights of the cathedral ceiling of the airport, and we fade into the bright white light—where we find, of course, the AT&T logo and contact information.

This is moving, if somewhat bizarre. And the religious iconography here does something more to explain the emotional power of the commercial.

How does this tie back to the other narrative strands?

It acknowledges—*vividly*, even blasphemously—the pain that work and separation from family cause us. How do men *feel* when we can't be with our children?

We feel as if we are being crucified.

But the appropriate response, apparently, is *not* fighting for fundamental change—this is *not* Liberation Theology, after all. Much more resonant here is Marx's characterization of religion as "the opiate of the masses."

Rather than fight for change, the logic of the commercial tells us we should accept that no heaven exists on earth, that our reward will come later, even that our suffering awards us some dignity, and that we must make the best of difficult circumstances.

In recent years, frequent business travelers have taken to calling themselves Road Warriors, sometimes with rueful humor, sometimes with pride. And AT&T Wireless, of course, is *at our service* to help us soldier on.

A Shrinking Market for Images of Inept Fathers?

Casting men—especially fathers and husbands—as objects of ridicule and their actions as comedic is nowhere *near* new. While the idea that women are flighty and emotional and men are responsible and rational is an ancient one, so is its mirror image: a picture of men as emotionally stunted to the point of insensitivity and prone to bouts of violence, easily diverted by sex, food, and leisure. In that latter scenario— particularly when it comes to home and hearth—women are the calm, efficient counterweight to irresponsible men.

The plays of William Shakespeare contain a number of such men— many of them less kings of their castles than they are court jesters: Lear in his famous mad scene, Polonius in *Hamlet*. Aristophanes' antiwar comedy *Lysistrata*, written in 411 B.C.E., revolves around Greek women staging a sex strike to pull their men back from the pointless violence of war.

Why has the Doofus Dad been such a staple of television advertising, and why might he be in the process of becoming a less compelling and effective device?

The appeal—the commercial efficacy—of this approach rests on a few basic principles:

1. Poking fun at a powerful person, or category of people, is funnier than attacking a weaker person or group of people.
2. Where men earn most or all of the money but women are responsible for a majority of the day-to-day domestic purchasing decisions, flattering women by ridiculing men is an effective way of appealing to "the household purchasing agent."
3. If men don't *want* a meaningful—or at any rate labor intensive—role in taking care of kids, cooking, and cleaning, they don't necessarily mind being represented as inept in these areas; this amounts to making fun of them for being substantially incapable of doing work that they don't want to do anyway.

If we accept those premises, the kinds of nascent social, cultural, and economic changes we have seen in the last generation or more offer a clear argument for why domestically inept men in general, and fathers in particular, *might* now be a bit less funny and a bit less effective as marketing tools—and why the backlash against the Doofus Dad may be growing:

1. While we don't have gender equality yet in the United States—however defined—the male monopoly on power has been broken.
2. While women still do the majority of the domestic shopping—for groceries and children's clothing, for example—there has been a substantial increase both in households where men are the principal purchasers of such items[4] and households in which these duties are shared to one degree or another.

3. The amount of time that men devote to kids, cooking, and cleaning has also increased, as has the number of households in which fathers are either primary or equally sharing parents.[5]

Moreover, an increasing variety of active campaigns have sprung up to discourage this sort of stereotyping of fathers. Some of this has come in the form of actions initiated by blogs or Web sites run by active fathers. Some has come from more formal organizations and movements. Some has come in the form of explicitly and purposefully positive advertising, not merely for products but for fathers.

In 2005, for example, the National Fatherhood Initiative and the Ad Council, as part of an ongoing collaboration, produced a series of TV ads—public service announcements or PSAs—in support of fathers taking a more active role in their children's lives.

The "Moments" campaign consisted of three thirty-second ads: "Dance," which shows a white man in his late thirties or early forties, dancing in his living room, in slacks, a button-down shirt, and a loosened tie—only at the end do we see that he is doing a dance routine with his young daughter; "Errand," in which an African American man is shown purchasing tampons and then bringing them to his teenaged daughter, who is waiting in the car; and "Lightsaber," which shows a white man out in his yard, in what looks like his bathrobe and pajamas, enthusiastically slicing the air with the kind of sword used by the Jedi Knights in the Star Wars saga and making childlike sounds of warfare—there too, the camera pulls back at the end to show us that he has been playing with his child.

All of the commercials end with Tom Selleck, off screen—a macho man and a conservative—giving the tag line: "The smallest moments can have the biggest impact on a child's life. It takes a *man* to be a dad."

All of the commercials center on a father doing something potentially embarrassing with or for his child. In effect, they tell men that *it's cool to be uncool for your kid.*

Most important, all of them include a character who looks on in something between bafflement and disapproval—the character who, as viewers, we are meant to react *against*, the character who may represent not merely mainstream hesitance to accept a more nurturing version of masculinity but our own ambivalence about the softer side of fatherhood as well, whether that ambivalence resides in men or in women reticent to embrace change.

A particularly interesting aspect of that last ad is that it echoes—in some ways it feels like it responds to—the Honda ad in which the father appears more concerned about his car than about his child. As the father with the lightsaber is jumping around the yard with his son, a nearby neighbor is waxing his car and looking on, somewhat stupefied by the spectacle.

Here, it is the man invested in lovingly taking care of his car whose priorities we are meant to see as empty. The dad in the bathrobe is surely an amusing sight, but we smile *with* him; we don't laugh *at* him. We admire him.

This grown man, who has very publicly thrown dignity to the wind to act like, and play with, his child, is doing the right thing.

9

Kevin Knussman: The Trooper Dad

*I would often get off [work] at 3:00 A.M. and get up
with kidly duties at 7:00, but that's part of the
commitment to raising your own kids.*

—KEVIN KNUSSMAN

"How many guns is too many?" Kevin asks. "A dozen? Fifteen?"
So Kevin has over a dozen guns in his house.

In the back seat of the car, Kevin's daughters, Paige and
Hope, both of them chubby cheeked, have fallen asleep, belted in but
slightly aslant. We've spent the better part of a stunningly hot afternoon at the Elks Club swimming pool, and though he slathered them
with sunscreen they've both gone slightly pink.

Now, having returned a few books and videos to the local library,
Kevin is driving me around their town—Easton, on Maryland's Eastern Shore—in the family's brown Mazda 929, which has over two
hundred thousand miles on it, the air conditioning humming gamely
as he shows me the lay of the land while we talk.

Yes, I think that's too many guns.

I hesitate for a moment before giving this answer. But really I have
no choice. He already knows my thinking on the topic: Left to my own
devices, I'd pretty much ban hand guns. And he's a Second Amendment absolutist: The way he puts it, he sees constitutional protection for
having an Uzi in the trunk of your car if that's what you want.

He's teasing me a little but perhaps testing me as well.

How much will I buffer my response to suit him?

"Yeah, that's too many guns to have at home," I tell him.

He smiles. I hope I'm getting points for honesty.

Kevin has better reasons than most other people with a private arsenal of that size: Guns were an important part of his professional life. He's a former Maryland State Trooper; a good number of those guns are retired service weapons. He's also a hunter. He grew up—not far from where he is now raising his own children—hunting game, in the 1960s and 1970s, a time when it wouldn't have been unusual for high schoolers to throw a shotgun into the trunk of the car before school so they could go hunting in the afternoon; he took a hunting hiatus for a number of years but went back to it in 2005, with Paige, then ten years old, after she completed a Hunter Safety Course.[1]

Although they make an interesting aside, I haven't come to Maryland to talk to Kevin about guns. More important than the conversation in the front seat are the kids asleep in the back seat, particularly Kevin's older daughter, Riley Paige.

Ultimately, Paige is the reason Kevin's most recent service weapons were retired. It was her birth that triggered the series of events that led to her father's separating from the Maryland State Police earlier than he would have liked, after a brutal and bruising series of lawsuits and appeals centered on the Federal Family and Medical Leave Act (FMLA) of 1993, the first measure President Bill Clinton signed into law on taking office.

In 1995, Howard Kevin Knussman became the first man to allege gender discrimination in the interpretation of the FMLA, over the state's refusal to give him leave to take care of his family after his wife, Kim, gave birth to Paige, having suffered complications that required her to be hospitalized for the preceding two weeks, and then came home in a debilitated condition.

Jill Mullineaux, the personnel manager of the Maryland State Police, couched the refusal this way: "Unless your wife is in a coma or dead, you can't be primary care provider" (and thus, to her way of thinking, eligible for family leave).

She reasoned, "You must be able to breast-feed a baby in order to be declared a primary care [PC] provider, and since you can't breast-feed, you can't possibly be a PC provider."[2]

The American Civil Liberties Union saw the matter a little differently, as, eventually, would the federal courts. But getting anything that remotely resembled justice—or, for that matter, resolution—would take more than a decade from the time Kevin first filed suit, in April 1995.

In February 1999, following an eleven-day trial and two hours of deliberation, a federal district court jury in Baltimore awarded Kevin $375,000 in compensatory damages. The state appealed this verdict to the Fourth Circuit Court of Appeals and was successful, some two years later, in having the award overturned. The judgment in Kevin's favor stood; the question of the amount was sent back down to be reheard.

All parties waived another jury trial, opting instead to allow the judge who had presided over the original trial to make the determination of damages. In the summer of 2002, Kevin was awarded a drastically reduced $40,000 in compensatory damages but over $600,000 in attorney's fees and court costs. The state paid the $40,000 but promptly appealed the costs judgment. The Fourth Circuit vacated the award of fees in its entirety, sending *that* aspect of the case back down to the district court in Baltimore.

By that time, the judge who had originally heard the case had retired.

And so it went.

Three years into retirement when we first met, only in his midforties, Kevin still *looks* like a state trooper. He has that bearing. Just over six feet, hair thinning just a bit, prescription aviator glasses, he still runs, still lifts weights—the local YMCA has a child-care room; he leans in slightly when you speak as some tall people tend to, taking in what you say, polite, interested, sometimes amused, nodding, thinking things over but not necessarily changing his mind.

You wouldn't want him leaning against your car door, asking for your license and registration; he has that unflappable focus that you don't want aimed at you if you've done something wrong. On the other hand, he spent the last eighteen of his twenty-three years with the state police as a helicopter paramedic, and he would be a reassuring sight coming toward you through the rotor backwash—medical kit in hand, hair awhirl in the breeze—to render aid and assistance. You'd want someone calm and focused then.

Kevin still shakes his head and smiles over the irony and the serendipity of a state trooper turning to the ACLU for legal help. So does attorney Debbie Jeon, one of the team of lawyers who spent years fighting on Kevin's behalf.

In addition to his own family's struggles, Kevin remains keenly aware of the toll—both financial and familial—that ten years of litigation took on the attorneys who fought for him. Maryland attorney Robin Cockey worked on a pro bono basis for most of that time; the ACLU's Debbie Jeon in the Maryland office and Sara Mandelbaum with the Women's Rights Project of the ACLU in New York City were also with him through the entire fight.

"They simply stood there, like a rock!" Kevin says. "They promised and delivered unwavering support for me and my family. All three attorneys put their hearts into ten years of bringing us justice."

You can read in the legal documents generated by the case that same fascinating hybrid of ideas—confounding easy "left versus right," "liberal versus conservative" labels—that Kevin's attitudes bespeak. Often, as in the following excerpt from an appellate brief, the best way to characterize the tone is "Libertarian."

I like the Libertarians; I think of them as one of the points on the political spectrum that bends back on itself, where the far left and the far right go to such extremes that they meet around back.

"This case," his attorneys wrote, "is about 'family values' in the truest sense. It is about one father struggling to honor his family commitments, against a tangle of bureaucrats who rank government protocol above the rights of citizens. Kevin Knussman is a conservative Christian who prizes his family and his faith above all—above even his once-cherished career as a Maryland State Trooper. He has paid a steep price for his priorities."[3]

In Kevin's view, a key part of the problem was that state government was too powerful; the representatives of the law—and of various layers of the public bureaucracy—believed themselves to be above the law.

Kevin was *not* the first police officer to face ridicule and rejection in such circumstances. Some eleven years before passage of the relevant federal law, Buffalo, New York, Police Lieutenant Timothy Scioli, whose wife was due to give birth in a few days, applied for time off under his department's "maternity leave" policy.

According to a *New York Times* article published in May 1982, James Cunningham, Buffalo's police commissioner, asked Lieutenant Scioli to furnish medical proof from a doctor that he was pregnant.

"Gynecology is not my field and we have no command officers in this department who are schooled in that," the *Times* quotes Cunningham as saying. "If he's pregnant, he'll get his leave."[4]

Kevin Knussman, of course, wasn't asking for "maternity leave." He was asking for "family leave," a distinction both of language and of law.

Eventually—after the birth of their second child, Hope, the legal case still wending its way through the courts—Kevin left the police force and became a stay-at-home father. In the years between the point at which he first filed suit and the time he retired, the Maryland State Police fought Kevin tenaciously.

Even after the Maryland State Police decided that leave would be granted to troopers in the same situation in the future, they refused to settle with Kevin. He was granted Primary Care Provider status, and twelve weeks off, after Hope's birth, but they still refused to admit they had been wrong the first time around, with Paige.

He was transferred to a facility significantly farther from his home. They grounded him, arguing that he was psychiatrically unfit to fly—an interesting and disturbing real-life echo of the father in *Mary Poppins*. Kevin was fighting to take care of his wife and daughter; that made his mental status suspect.

"There was nothing in the trial testimony to indicate a need to remove me from flying," Kevin says, "especially when I still had my badge, gun, and police car."

He had been depressed, he says, but that was a condition that he had worked through and that, at any rate, had been at its strongest during the transfer, the legal maneuvers, and other forms of pretrial harassment.

"During and after the trial," he says, "I was perfectly okay."

The state's primary focus was on making the job he had always loved untenable. He would never fly medevacs again.

When state law was amended to allow troopers with twenty-two years of service to retire with a full pension—with twenty-three years in—Kevin welcomed the opportunity.

As Kevin saw it, much of this was straight retribution. One of their own had filed—and won—a high-profile lawsuit; there had been national media attention, including Kevin's appearance on *Good Morning America*.

Any police force is a paramilitary organization, and it operates by many of the rules and procedures, written and just as crucially unwritten, that govern the armed forces. Discipline is important, as is unit cohesion. You follow the command mast when you have a problem—which is to say you don't go over anybody's head. But, more important, you don't *have* problems, because that's whining. And, at the top of the list, you don't air the institution's dirty laundry in public. An integral part of that credo is a rhetoric of family that is written into how we talk about these kinds of organizations and how they talk about themselves, again both officially and unofficially: as brothers in arms—or, in the case of the police, as brother officers; police officers often band together in professional organizations with names like "The Fraternal Order of Law Enforcement Officers."

When Family Comes into Conflict with Family

Kevin has an accent with notes in it that you can hear from southern New Jersey and eastern Pennsylvania down into Maryland—where he grew up, in Denton, in nearby Caroline County—a tendency to swirl sounds together: Baltimore becomes *Ballamore,* just as denizens of Philadelphia often refer to one of their city's main daily newspapers as *The Fluffyia Ink Wire.*

Earlier, we'd sat at a table by the side of the pool, Paige, then seven, and Hope, then five, in and out of the water, back and forth between us and the pool, intermittently curious about the tape recorder but generally more focused on pool toys and Strawberry Newtons and when the grownups were coming into the water to play.

Kevin parsed the almost seven years of legal, political, and emotional wrangling for me. He was relatively calm about it. Legally, issues had yet to be resolved—he had won a settlement of $375,000 in the first trial, but that was being appealed, and how much he would end up with versus how much would go to his attorneys was an open question. Emotionally, however, his family had already walked through the fire. In many ways, from his perspective, whatever was to come would be mostly epilogue.

When I stayed home to take care of my daughter, I had a ponytail. And I'm the sort of person you might expect to be a stay-at-home dad: a middle-class, left-wing academic. (I can put myself in those boxes when it constitutes efficient shorthand; when someone else does it, it's offensively reductive.)

When Kevin retired from the Maryland State Police and became a stay-at-home Dad, Kim teased him about whether *he* was going to grow a ponytail.

Not the slightest chance in the world.

But, labels and stylistic cues aside, Kevin's family probably constitutes a more representative example of how family life has changed—of how the role, or acceptable *range* of roles, of fatherhood has changed, and will likely continue to change, than does the example of my own family.

Research suggests that people like me are more likely to talk a good line about sharing domestic labor and then to put their children in day care—which, I'll concede here as a matter of full disclosure, is what we did, at least part-time, when our daughter was two and a half and I went back to school to pursue my doctorate.

Arguably, in the category of "equally sharing parents," where the fathers do as much as the mothers—to care for kids, to cook, to keep house, and to hold down jobs as well—more culturally conservative families are in the vanguard.

But this trend is close to invisible. Families in which the parents do shift work—police officers, firefighters, utility workers, nurses— often don't have the income to pay for day care. Perhaps more important, for the most part, they don't *believe* in day care; they believe in families caring for kids.

Family values, remember?

I've already alluded to psychologist Francine Deutsch, a professor at Mount Holyoke College, and the observations she makes about these changes in her 1999 book, *Halving It All: How Shared Parenting Works.* One reason that changes in these families are less visible, her research suggests, is the stigma, as much self-perceived as anything else, that often attaches to parents in conservative shift-working households. The mothers are afraid of being seen as "shirking their duty to their children and their husbands," and the fathers are afraid to be seen as "giving in and doing *women's work.*"[5]

So this change has stayed under the radar. Increasingly, the traditional value of taking care of one's family is trumping traditional family structure. But I believe the families that do this most are talking about it least. Perhaps the greatest effect of these changes will be seen when the generation now being raised in quietly egalitarian households is old enough to begin forming their own families.

Whom they want to be with, how they want to configure their households and divide up the work, how they will define the roles of fathers and mothers, all of this is more likely to be informed by what they experienced when they were growing up—Dad and Mom trading off cooking, cleaning, and child care, everyone pitching in to do whatever was necessary—rather than by traditional ideas, rather than rhetoric, about who is *supposed* to do what.

At the Elks Club pool, I had asked Kevin if or when he might return to some kind of full-time work; at that point he was serving as a part-time paramedic once or twice per week.

He would consider it, he told me, when his younger daughter was out of high school. Both of his children were going to need more parental contact and supervision as they got older, he said, not less. He wanted to be there for them.

I felt a little twinge of embarrassment at this, my sensitive progressive credentials tarnished; maybe I'm not as a good a father as I like to think. Kevin's viewpoint was an interesting and powerful alloy of conservative and radical thinking: His sense that children need a parent to take care of them was even keener than mine, but he didn't care whether that parent was the mother or the father. (Several years later, in July 2005, Kevin would accept full-time work as a paramedic. But his schedule would allow him to continue to be at home to take care of his children three out of every four days.)

A few weeks prior to our conversation, a study had come out on the positive social, developmental, and academic impact of a mother staying home during her children's first few years. It's the kind of research and the kind of news program sound bite that drives me crazy on a regular basis: fathers are simply invisible; almost no one seems to think of looking at these questions in a gender-neutral fashion, to ask about the impact of there being a stay-at-home *parent*.

I mention this to Kevin and he laughs in agreement; he'd heard about the same study.

"They never mentioned in there what the impact is if mom goes back to work but dad stays home. I tend to think that it's not so important that mom stays home; it's important that *somebody* stays home and takes care of the kids and that that person is engaged in providing a nurturing and loving and educational environment. I'd be curious to see a study that did that. And I would be willing to bet that there is no difference whether the mother or the father stays home."

The Knussmans don't like to be described as "Conservative Christians." They *are* both conservative and Christian, but neither of them likes to be labeled, to have their beliefs boiled down and put into neat little boxes.

At breakfast the following day, Kim tells me, "They think you're a Bible thumper [when you put Conservative and Christian together]. . . . We are certainly not perfect people and we would not want people to think we just are these pious people who look down their noses at others. That isn't what we want to do or project. . . . We go to church but we try to *live* what we are taught as much as we can, and we want our kids to be brought up that way."

They're right. They don't fit in the box. But maybe nobody does anymore.

Norman Rockwell Country

Downtown Easton, the county seat of Talbot County, on Maryland's Eastern Shore, gives the initial impression of being pleasantly frozen in time, but in fact it was both remade and thrown *back* in time in the 1950s, with Colonial Williamsburg as an overt model.

It was an early example of the kind of zoning and economic development that has since become common. And it probably succeeded better than most for being among the first.

The zoning laws that helped remake the town center were not overwhelmingly popular at the outset. In the 1950s, during the local debate over these changes, the idea of restricting what people could do with their property was compared unfavorably to Stalinism. But the present-day result is quite appealing. The downtown is a clean core area of several square blocks, largely built around the courthouse and a municipal complex. There's good, off-street parking; the sidewalks are clean; at the outer edges, the new buildings, though stylistically more modern, blend in with the dominant red brick theme.

Easton is no bastion of liberalism, and it never was. A statue stands in front of the courthouse, a Rebel soldier with a discreetly indistinct banner and the inscription "To the Talbot Boys 1861–1865 C.S.A." And then, in front of the statue, planted in the dirt—in this context and to northern eyes, both slightly dissonant and mildly reassuring—

a small American flag. (A few years later it was decided that the Talbot Boys would be joined by a statue of Frederick Douglass, and fund-raising to accomplish this goal began.)

Several blocks away, at the upscale Tidewater Inn, a brass plaque is embedded in the brickwork sidewalk out front, commemorating the fiftieth anniversary of Rotary International, noting the founding of the local club in 1921. A fleur de lis points north, and a series of city names and distances let you know that—among other things—you are 230 miles from New York, 2,828 miles from Los Angeles, 8,629 miles from Bombay, and 10,067 miles from Canberra.

Moving out from the core, both Easton and Talbot County are a complicated mix: Dilapidated living room furniture on sagging front porches contrasts with isolated mansions that boast their own docks, backdoor access to the Choptank River or the Chesapeake Bay. They have one of the highest concentrations of millionaires in the country, along with small farmers hurt by recent drought.

Highway 50, which cuts through town, is bordered by cornfields for good stretches of the Mid-Shore, the monotony of the green inter-rupted by the occasional farm stand or someone selling barbecue that's being cooked on a grill formed from a bisected oil drum. Where it cuts through Easton's eastern quarter, the highway has been colonized by strip malls, hotels, and Big Box Retail, which can bring you to a near-standstill if you attempt to brave traffic at the wrong time of day.

These growing pains notwithstanding, it's an appealing place to live and to raise a family: good schools—including the Christian school where the Knussmans send their daughters—fine scenery, and a pleth-ora of recreational opportunities, no shortage of shopping or amenities.

The draw of the area remains strong enough that some people choose to live there and commute as far as Baltimore or Washington, both about seventy miles away, ninety minutes or so when traffic is light—though traffic is rarely light. Kim Knussman commutes to An-napolis, to her job as an accounting manager with the Department of Natural Resources, about an hour away, just over the Chesapeake Bay Bridge.

More Room to Fold Clothes

Kevin laughs a little ruefully.

Yes, *any day now*, he's going to build himself a workbench along one wall of his two-car garage—in that space currently occupied by the family's third vehicle, a pick-up truck that's started to rust and really shouldn't be outside anymore, which he mostly only uses now to drive to the dump.

Kim smiles at this plan as well. She is slightly heavyset, with a round face, neatly styled short, reddish hair, and glasses. If Kevin most often seems philosophical when talking about what his family has been through, Kim evinces the occasional flash of anger.

Their house is a modern two-story with beige siding, light and spacious inside, crucifixes on the walls in a couple of the downstairs rooms. The back yard looks almost the size of a football field, a small shed in the far corner, a sturdy wooden picnic table, along with a swing and slide set in the middle distance. The long, hot, dry summer has turned the grass uniformly straw colored, with only one or two small patches of green.

The business about the workbench is amusing because Kevin's been "about to get to this" roughly since they had the house built, some ten years earlier. And anyway, these days, when they talk about having work done on the house, his priorities lie in other directions.

"Yeah, if we were planning the house now," he says, "I'd want a bigger kitchen, a bigger washroom. You need more room to fold clothes. I didn't know that then."

He knows it now.

The Knussmans have spent more than a decade struggling to juggle child care and work, to run their household, to take care of their children.

Before Kevin retired, Kim worked a half-time job on his days off. He worked four ten-hour days and had three days off; Kim worked two ten-hour days when Kevin was at home.

Three mornings a week or so, in the winter, Kevin would use the preschool day-care facility at the YMCA to give himself an hour and a half for a workout and a shower.

"No ONE in their 'RIGHT' or 'LEFT' mind," he wrote me recently, "would not use some relief from the kids!"

They did this from 1994 until July 1999 when he retired.

"No easy task," Kevin says, "given I would often get off at 3:00 A.M. and get up with kidly duties at 7:00, but that's part of the commitment to raising your own kids."

In July 2005, Kevin took a full-time position as a paramedic in Caroline. He works one or two days each week on a twenty-four-hours-on/three-days-off rotation, knows his schedule for a year in advance, and has the flexibility to switch days when he has to—switching a weekday for a weekend day to work around Kim's schedule, for kid's activities, school holidays, and so on. They use the school secretary to watch the kids until 5:30, and Kim goes in early on those days in order to get home in time for pickup.

"I'm still at home with the kids three out of every four days," Kevin says, "and I do almost all the cooking, cleaning, and shopping."

The cooking and the laundry are easier now than in the past: Subsequent to my visit, they've remodeled their downstairs to include a much larger kitchen and a dramatically larger utility room. They also traded in the old truck for one better able to withstand the elements, making room for Kevin to finally get that workbench he'd been talking about for so long.

It's interesting that a man who has spent his life in a quintessentially masculine profession is now so comfortable as a nurturing parent, so comfortable not only doing housework but also *talking* about it. But maybe that's exactly the point. It makes intuitive sense—in a Nixon-to-China[6] kind of way—that we might ultimately see the most progress from a fairly conservative corner: Hippy, progressive fathers, with their children in backpacks and Snuglis, aren't news, after all, and arguably did as much to keep caretaking fathers *out* of the mainstream as they did to bring them in.

Trooper Dad, on the other hand—the media tag Kevin picked up during his long legal battle—is an image likely to bring more mainstream and more conservative "active" fathers out of the closet.

Recent history may be moving us in this direction as well.

One of the effects that we saw in the aftermath of 9/11 was a level of public display of emotion on the part of American men that we haven't often seen. Most commonly, for obvious reasons, the men we saw were first responders: police officers, firefighters, paramedics. They were the ones most deeply involved in the ongoing tragedy and trauma in the first few days—at Ground Zero, at the Pentagon, at the crash site in Pennsylvania; they were the ones for whom the loss of comrades was most immediate and most obvious. And no one suggested that there was anything unmanly in those displays.

There was a strong family component to the sense of loss experienced by the first responders: they work in buildings they call "houses," where they often live and eat together during extended shifts; they routinely use the rhetoric of family to describe their bonds; as previously noted, they belong to unions and other organizations referred to as "brotherhoods" and "fraternal" orders. Family was a recurrent theme in the *New York Times* series "Portraits of Grief," which ran for months after 9/11, providing biographical snapshots of the lives lost. Invariably, they stressed the relationships that the first responders, most of them men, had enjoyed with their children.

These portraits were not just boilerplate phrases about how much they loved their children. They were detailed and specific, about deep connections, shared activities, time spent together, time they spent caring *for* their kids, not just caring about them—perhaps a fast first glimpse of the kinds of changes in family life Deutsch wrote about.

We may write that off to the gentle buffing out of scratches and blemishes that we often employ when we look back on people's lives. This is anecdotal observation, not statistical analysis. But we may also be seeing a shift in what it means to be a father, in the range of possibilities for that role, and for the broader role of "being a man."

And those changes don't always come from the directions we expect them to.

Epilogue

. . . .

I n writing these stories and in looking at how media have sometimes worked to slow social change, sometimes worked to help it along, sometimes merely reflected what has been happening in our culture, I'm after contradictory goals—both politically and emotionally.

I want men who are taking a role in caring for their children— whether as primary parents or as co-parents—to be acknowledged.

Look at us!

At almost the same time, to pay too much attention to men in this situation borders on disrespect and insult. It provides short-term gratification but ultimately isn't useful.

What are you looking at?

While something between ironic and amusing, this contradiction isn't new or unique. It's closer to being a developmental phase, really.

American civil rights movements—for African Americans, for women, for gay people, among others—have often supplemented their political goals with cultural goals. In addition to looking forward, to a future of accomplishment and inclusion, and saying, "This is where we want or deserve to be," they've also looked back, on historical accounts that have painted them out of the picture, and said, "We've been here for a long time and haven't been acknowledged for what we've done."

This has meant, for example, that in 1970, an educator might say, "It is crucial that we make a place in our history books to highlight the accomplishments of Charles Drew. People need to know that an African American can be an important physician and researcher."

Today, to say that "an African American can be an important physician and researcher" has a condescending ring to it. If you really believe in equality, why make a show of recognizing race or gender or sexual orientation?

It was progress in 1970 to notice; it represents progress as well that the "need to notice" is receding today.

Are *men* now claiming the mantle of oppressed group struggling for civil rights?

Some are.

But I'm neither marching nor huddled with the Angry White Men, railing about reverse discrimination. I'm down on the floor with the other parents, fretting about that (organic) grape juice stain and trying to find my daughter's earring back. I'm usually tired, sometimes frustrated, intermittently confused, but I'm not looking to do battle in the gender wars; I'm looking to work things out.

We need to stop thinking about issues of equality as competitive, as a zero-sum game, as wedge issues, as cudgels with which to beat each other for sins either past or present.

There is a moral imperative in the direction of justice, of equality of opportunity, of fairness, but there is a practical imperative as well: As a white person, I am diminished by racism in my society, my outlook narrowed and impoverished; as a straight man, my gender identity is crimped by homophobia; and as a man, my options are constrained by sexism.

We *all* have an interest in, a very real stake in, fairness; demanding justice for one group doesn't leave less justice for other groups.

That said, justice isn't a destination; it's a path: rocky in some places, smooth in others, sometimes a pleasure, sometimes a slog, and never ending.

Just when you think you've got the route all mapped out, the terrain changes.

Where We Are and Where We're Going

Why is it more and more common for *both* parents to actively participate in child care?[1]

The stories of the families we've looked at suggest several significant factors.

First and foremost, more men are taking care of their children *because we have to.*

The economic landscape in America has been remade in the last generation; the two-earner household is the norm—the only way for most families to keep themselves rooted, however tenuously, in the middle class.

Call this leveling of the playing field in the economic and the professional spheres a victory for feminists and egalitarians.

Call it a rare, happy side-effect of the damage wrought by unfettered capitalism and globalism on the march. *That's* an ironic marriage: Both feminism—at least equity feminism, its egalitarian strand—and capitalism value interchangeability.

Call it the cultural analogue to Newton's Third Law of Motion: "For every action, there is an equal and opposite reaction."

Economic and cultural change has created something of a vacuum around child care—real and imagined—lamented both on the left and on the right. Women have been simultaneously leaping and being pulled into the workforce; as a consequence, men are being pulled—or are leaping—into the domestic sphere.

But, utility and economics aside for the moment, we are also taking care of our children for reasons not only of necessity or financial imperative but as a consequence of opportunity, *because we can.*

Economic need has *required* more participation; cultural change has *permitted* more participation; that latter piece, the matter of permission, is meaningful only because there is also a *desire* on the part of many men to have more nurturing relationships with their children.

A cultural space has begun to appear—small, irregular, spasming open and closed from time to time and place to place—in which it is at least sometimes recognized as acceptable, sometimes desirable, sometimes *necessary*, for men to openly demonstrate our softer side. We can see this in how the language of parenting is beginning to change. We can see it in the growing range of representations of men in general and fathers in specific: on television, in movies, and in advertising.

This role flexibility has been slower and more tentative in emerging for men than it has for women—and I say that while fully acknowledging what a long and difficult struggle the latter has been. As I have already written, women were fighting their way into a more powerful position; men who seek or accept either an equal role or the primary role with children are often deemed to be shirking, or shrinking from masculine responsibilities, while invading women's territory to boot, their motives suspect on all sides.

We can—and of course we *do*, both among and between the genders—argue about whether or not men are doing enough and about what "enough" means. Nature, nurture, genetics, biology, wiring, hormones, and brain anatomy notwithstanding, however, we *are* caring for our children.

As to barriers . . . Back again to the matter of territoriality.

We can—and we *should*—argue about, or at least, in an ongoing way, discuss, what we think constitutes positive and effective parenting.

I don't mind being judged, even if I am sometimes found lacking.

Tell me that I have in some way been a bad parent and—albeit grumpily—I am willing to listen to and at least consider criticism. Tell me that I have been a bad parent because "men just don't get it," and I'm not going to hear much of anything that comes after that.

Like anyone else, I am a hybrid, a member of any number of groups; I can be categorized and described in myriad ways. It isn't that I don't feel that you can make statistically reasonable generalizations about men or women, about religious groups, sexual orientation, ethnic origin. It is that I am not the sum of my group memberships; none of us are.

Few people, at this point, would look at an African American lesbian and assess her job performance—as a lawyer, a carpenter, or a mother—on the basis of her race, gender, or sexual orientation. That's not a matter of political correctness, but of ethics, etiquette, and law.

Men deserve the same.

The issue is not that we cannot or should not judge people. We judge people all the time, and we have a clear societal interest in judging whether or not people do an adequate job of taking care of children.

The issue is *how* we judge people, by what standards, using what benchmarks, with what degree of consistency.

What we ought to privilege are functional results.

Some would argue that "a *good* family is a functional family."

But down the centuries—and with a vengeance in the United States in the last few decades—tagging some families as good has been a way to tag others as bad. I have no problem with families consisting of a churchgoing heterosexual couple and their biological children—mom in the kitchen and dad at work. If they're happy, I'm happy for them.

But I am unwilling to define family values based on trying to pin down what we mean by "good," whether that has to do with perceived morals, with family composition, or with any other externally imposed benchmark.

Rather, I would reverse the terms: "A *functional* family is a good family."

It's a bit easier—though still not without controversy—to agree on a rough, shared definition of "functional" than of "good."

Do the people in a given household consider each other family?

Are they taking care of each other?

If it works for them, it works for me.

Just as women have been experiencing, in growing numbers and with increasing intensity, both the pleasures and the pains of a fuller palette of work and professional situations than ever before, men are experiencing—and often seeking out—the reciprocal set of joys and frustrations on the home front, with our children at the top of the list.

And just as there has been an effort over the past generation to reconsider the workplace in light of what some feminists have referred to as "women's ways of being and ways of knowing," a greater male presence in child care requires a reciprocal process.

What it means to be a man is beginning to open up in the same way that *what it means to be a woman* has opened up. Both of those changes, that destabilization of roles, scare and outrage some people. Having the clarity of "the right way to do things" replaced by a dizzying menu of options can be confusing, but freedom is a good problem to have.

The more of us taking care of our children, the better.

Afterword

· · · · · · · ·

GROW UP

I miss her already, my daughter
Two years old and slick as a seal with me
* in our claw foot tub*
Swimming away, upward toward the light

And when I say I cut the cord
* changed-you-bathed-you-fed-you*
Oh Dad, she'll sigh, exasperated
Let it go, will you?

Grow up

And—if I want that for either of us
* I can't quite figure out which one*

—Originally published in *Worcester Magazine,*
August 8, 1997, by this author

Fourteen years old now, my daughter still glides up and down the Merritt Parkway with me, down to New York, back up to Massachusetts. When it's just the two of us in the car, she sits up front, often texting on her Blackberry. These days I teach at MIT, a much more manageable commute—lots of parents on the Writing across the Curriculum staff and a commitment, robust and gender-neutral, to help each other integrate family with work as smoothly as possible.

She's still here, Rebecca (*Beckie!*). But—as I knew I would—I miss her.

I never expected to be Super Dad, and I'm not. Whenever I give public presentations that revolve around fathering issues, I half expect my wife or daughter to pop up in the back of the room and offer a counterpoint.

Yeah, he talks *a good line, but listen—*

We work within, we wrestle and negotiate with, our limitations; we do the best we can. I'm sure I would parent somewhat differently if given the chance to start over, but I'm less sure about the details of what I would change.

Starting over isn't on offer, anyway.

I'm proud of my daughter. I'm proud of my wife. I'm proud of myself, too, though I feel something between arrogant and sheepish making that last assertion.

We all have a limited capacity to achieve the results we aim for. But what I think my wife and I deserve the most credit for, as parents and as partners, is our aim, our *intentionality*. We've succeeded where we've succeeded; we've failed where we've failed; further chapters remain to be written. But we have planned and researched and argued and negotiated and compromised; we have dug in and we have let go; we have looked at each other or at our child and thrown our hands up in exasperation and we have smiled in wordless wonder; we've juggled work and marriage and parenthood and making our household run; and we've dropped the occasional flaming torch on the living room carpet.

The closest I'll come to a formula is to say that you have to ask, often and seriously, "How do *we* want *our* family to work?" And you have to be able—with grace and calm, neither my strong suit—to do something between gently rejecting and quietly ignoring the list of rules and regulations unrelentingly pressed upon you by friends, family, schools, religious authorities, and bystanders both well meaning and malign.

As to my daughter, well, a few years back . . .

We were in the car, of course—*driving, driving, always driving*—talking about her upcoming birthday and party. Her circle of friends were in an admirable cycle; rather than asking people to give presents, they would designate a charity and suggest donations.

Which charity did she want people to donate to?

She'd had a pet rabbit for a while by then; she wanted the money to go to a pet rabbit charity.

"What am I going to say about this?" I asked her, and she didn't hesitate.

"Take care of the humans first."

"Right," I said.

Save the cute! has bothered me for a long time. Peace be upon all pet owners, but I don't understand how we spend $20 billion per year on medical care for pets while upward of 45 million Americans have no health care—our pet med expenditure could insure 4 million people.

"Are you going to let me do that?"

"It's your choice," I told her.

And, indeed, that's what she ended up doing.

But *I'm in her head*, just as I have family voices in my head— primary among them that of my grandmother, for whom my daughter was named, who sometimes offers praise, sometimes admonition, whose counsel I sometimes heed, sometimes ignore—and I don't think we can do much better than that as parents. It's *catch and release*, from birth to independence. We don't get to follow them around forever; we hope that some of our words, our ideas, our values, will.

And they teach us too.

"You should shave before you come to help with swimming lessons," she told me when she was three years old. "Then you might scare some of the other kids less."

I should shave, even though I'm not going to work!

I should think about how my appearance makes other people feel!

I should consider the possibility that people of different ages might re-act in different ways!

Fascinating.

Thank you.

Appendixes

· · · · · · · · ·

Appendix A: Comparative Word Frequency (2006 and 2009)

"Feminine intuition," 31,400 hits (ca. 95 percent)
"Masculine intuition," 1,610 hits (ca. 5 percent)

Google Search: September 3, 2006

"Feminine intuition," 102,000 hits (ca. 99.2 percent)
"Masculine intuition," 834 hits (ca. 0.8 percent)

Google Search: August 3, 2009[1]

Appendix B: AT&T Wireless Commercial, "Business Trip," Shot Sequence (Approximate)

For the most part, I have tried simply to describe what a viewer of the commercial sees, without editorializing or drawing conclusions. There are a few places where—in describing facial expressions or body language, for example—I've made some judgments about meaning; I've tried to keep this to an absolute minimum.

1. We see a man in a business suit, burdened with luggage, unsuccessfully attempt to insert a keycard into a hotel room door lock. The hallway walls are white; the carpets and the doors are red.

2. He kneels in the hallway, struggling with the keycard. To the left of his door, we see the edge of a glass case containing a message board: white plastic letters on black, felt furrows.

3. Door opens. Camera, from point of view (p.o.v.) inside the room, captures his reaction to the room. Over his shoulder, we can see that his room is right across from the elevator.

4. From his p.o.v., we see a bed with twin pillows, with twin light fixtures attached to the wall above the head of the bed. Both the walls and the blanket are gray.

5. We see him sitting on the edge of the mattress, at the foot of the bed, in shirt, boxer shorts, and socks. On his knees is a tray; on the tray is a large, white plate, which he has just revealed by lifting off a bell-like, metal cover. In the middle of the plate, dwarfed by everything around it, is some item of food—presumably a piece of meat—roughly the size of a deck of cards and elaborately garnished; he looks something between unimpressed and bewildered by this.

Behind him and to the right, one corner of the room is a glass cubicle, reflecting an image of the bed, doubling the effect of the twin pillows and lights. Through the glass, we can make out a toilet, a tile "tray" on the floor, and on the wall above this tray, the edge of something metallic—presumably a shower faucet. There are curtains, gathered in the corners of the cubicle but not pulled closed. All of this, along with the gray color scheme, makes the room look like an elegant prison.

6. We see him asleep on his back: arms straight out from his body, in scarecrow position; still in the same state of partial undress. We see this from above, the shot at an angle, his head pointed toward the bottom right of the shot and his legs toward the top left.

7. P.o.v. outside a yellow taxi, which is moving through a tunnel, away from the light at the entrance. We see his upper body, his head tilted back slightly as he looks upward with an exhausted, forlorn expression on his face.

8. He stands at an airport security checkpoint, arms straight out from his body, again in scarecrow position, as two people examine him, one with a metal-detecting wand.

9. We see him running through the airport, suitcase in one hand, garment bag in the other, newspaper under his arm.

10. From above, we see a bustling airport concourse, with him threading his way through the crowd.

11. We see a flight board, the third item flashing a red "Delayed" notice; the image of his upper body and face are reflected off the surface of the board as he turns away.

12. We see him sitting alone in a gate waiting area, looking at his watch; behind him, through large windows, we can see a jetway, attached to nothing, and empty tarmac.

13. We see his face from the side, turned away from us, as he blows out air in frustration and exhaustion. We hear a breathy little girl's voice:

Daughter: Hi, Daddy.

He turns toward the camera, his face lighting up and softening. He smiles and says:

Father: Hey, Sweetheart!

14. We cut to the face of a little girl, perhaps six or seven years old, curly blonde hair, blue eyes; she has her face tilted to the left, her cheek resting on her fist. The camera angle is from his p.o.v. and slightly behind, so that we can see a little bit of his head in the shot.

Father: I miss you.
Daughter: I miss you too.

Her hand opens from a fist to a palm that now cups the side of her face.

15. We pull back to a two-shot of father and daughter. She's sitting on the waiting-area chair immediately adjacent to his, legs folded underneath her, her left knee up and her arms clasped around it, leaning toward her father. She wears a red and blue soccer uniform, high socks over shin guards. In his seat, he is sitting facing forward, but with his head turned toward her, his body inclined in her direction; a wedding band is visible on his left hand.

Father: What did you do today?
Daughter: I played soccer.

As she says her line, other passengers materialize and begin to walk quickly back and forth between the scene we have been watching and the camera. The daughter dematerializes and we see instead only the father, sitting, smiling broadly, animated and talking into a cell phone.

Announcer: For your most important calls, Reach Out, on the wireless service America trusts: AT&T Wireless.

16. The camera pulls back as he continues to talk. He is still smiling and animated, though we do not hear his words. The row of chairs he is sitting on is on the airport's second tier, and people move along that row from left to right, and vice versa; on the tier below, they move along a corridor from the top of the shot to the bottom, and vice versa. He sits just above and to the right of the intersection of those two lines.

17. Camera moves up, from the second tier to the vaulted skylights above and the screen fades to white, on which is imposed the AT&T Wireless logo, 800 number, and Web address.

Appendix C: Comparative Word Frequency (2004 and 2006)

"Working mother," 140,000 hits (82 percent)
"Working parent," 25,800 hits (15 percent)
"Working father," 4,430 hits (3 percent)

"Soccer mom," 118,000 hits (94 percent)
"Soccer parent," 2,780 hits (4 percent)
"Soccer dad," 5,340 hits (2 percent)

"Stay-at-home mom," 75,300 hits (83 percent)
"Stay-at-home parent," 13,000 hits (14 percent)
"Stay-at-home dad," 2,400 hits (3 percent)

Google Search: October 6, 2004

"Working mother," 2,000,000 hits (83 percent)
"Working parent," 302,000 hits (13 percent)
"Working father," 97,000 hits (4 percent)

"Soccer mom," 1,610,000 hits (78 percent)
"Soccer parent," 24,200 hits (1 percent)
"Soccer dad," 436,000 hits (21 percent)

"Stay-at-home mom," 4,410,000 hits (88 percent)
"Stay-at-home parent," 169,000 hits (3 percent)
"Stay-at-home dad," 420,000 hits (8 percent)

Google Search: July 12, 2006

Notes

· · · · · · · ·

Introduction

1. Now known as Legal Momentum.

2. Mark Crispin Miller, "Getting Dirty," in *Boxed In: The Culture of TV* (Evanston, Ill.: Northwestern University Press, 1988), 401.

3. Oscar Lewis makes a similar argument in the introduction to *The Children of Sánchez*: "The independent versions of the same incidents given by various family members provide a built-in check upon the reliability and validity of much of the data and thereby partially offset the subjectivity inherent in a single autobiography" ([New York: Random House, 1961], xi).

4. See Molly Monahan Lang and Barbara J. Risman, "A 'Stalled' Revolution or a Still-Unfolding One?" Available at www.contemporaryfamilies.org/subtemplate .php?t=briefingPapers&ext=stalledrevolution. "Research by Robinson and Godbey shows that men spent more than 4 hours per week longer each week doing housework and child care in 1985 than they did in 1965. During the same period, women decreased their time doing such work by over 9 hours per week. Some people have claimed the revolution in gender behavior 'stalled' in the 1980s. But [b] etween 1985 and 2000, fathers continued to increase their time doing housework and child care, while mothers' time doing housework continued to decrease. Women still do more household labor than men, but they have been doing less every generation and every decade. In addition, men are much more likely than in the past to tell pollsters that they desire fewer hours in the labor force and more time for their family."

5. The Web site www.daycaresdontcare.org, for example, cites Jewish, Christian, and Moslem scriptures and history to argue that having children cared for outside the family is dangerous and contrary to religious tradition.

6. Psychologist Francine M. Deutsch, a professor at Mount Holyoke College, notes both these changes and the reticence about discussing them in her book *Halving It All: How Equally Shared Parenting Works* (Cambridge, Mass.: Harvard University Press, 1999).

7. For a year after the terrorist attacks of 9/11, the *New York Times* ran a series entitled "Portraits of Grief," which gave brief biographical sketches of people who had died. For obvious reasons, first responders—police officers, firefighters, and EMTs—were disproportionately represented. Anecdotally, there was significant and repeated emphasis on the consistent and concrete ways in which the men in this cohort were actively involved in taking care of their children. We may ascribe this in part to the sentimentality of obituaries, but it dovetails well with Deutsch's findings.

8. Refers to a 1972 song book and record album, produced by "Marlo Thomas and Friends," with the proceeds donated to the Ms. Foundation. In 1974, a TV special was spun off the album. The dominant theme, related to gender and other issues of difference, was "You can be anything you want to be."

9. Since 1991, women have outnumbered men in college. The U.S. Census Bureau's Current Population Survey put that advantage at 54 percent to 46 percent as of 2005. Large gap. Big problem. But, of course, it's not a competition. See www.census.gov/population/www/socdemo/school/cps2005.html.

10. Molly Haskell, "Hers," *New York Times*, February 11, 1982, p. C2.

11. Dr. Cathy Read, author of *Preventing Breast Cancer: The Politics of an Epidemic*, said, "The successes of AIDS activists convinced breast cancer survivors of the powers of political action. Not only have women adopted similar lobbying tactics. Many now talk of 'coming out' when they tell family and friends of a breast cancer diagnosis." See www.channel4.com/health/microsites/0-9/4health/sex/lgb_aids.html.

12. Several years ago, I gave a conference presentation on why men don't often take advantage of family leave policies ("Why Men Don't Take Family Leave: Why They Might," Modern Language Association Annual Convention, New York City, December 2002). During the Q&A that followed, one woman announced, "I don't want to hear anything about men and family leave until every woman has been guaranteed family leave!" It struck me as poor strategy to write off half of one's potential allies.

Chapter 1

1. The most recent U.S. Census Bureau data ("Parents and Children in Stay-at-Home Parent Family Groups: 1994 to Present, 2007") cites more than a doubling over the previous decade (1997–2007) of men leaving the workforce to care for their children, from 71,000 to 165,000—should one want to emphasize change.

This compares with circa 5.5 million stay-at-home mothers—should one want to emphasize stasis.

2. Sharon Hays, *The Cultural Contradictions of Motherhood* (New Haven, Conn.: Yale University Press, 1998), 103.

3. Clifford Geertz, *The Interpretation of Cultures* (New York: Basic Books, 1973), 36.

4. Ángel Nieto, *El Machinchar: Diálogo en Dos Voces* (New York: Scholastic, 1993), 5.

5. Ibid., 10.

6. Ibid., 13.

7. Ibid., 23.

8. "Revving Up for the Next Twenty Five Years." *Ms. Magazine,* September/October 1997, p. 83.

Chapter 2

1. The opening section of this chapter appeared in somewhat different form in Donald N. S. Unger, "When Fathers *Mother*," *Voice Male* (Summer 2000), p. 15.

2. Robin Lakoff, *Language and Woman's Place* (New York: Colophon Books, 1975), 28.

3. Dale Spender, *Man Made Language* (London: Routledge and Kegan Paul, 1985), 163.

4. See www.usconstitution.net/dream.html.

5. One example of this change would be the For Fathering Project, a nonprofit, public health program founded in 1997. The goals statement reads in part, "The For Fathering Project reflects the emerging national consensus that responsible fatherhood means much more than being present and providing economic support. Today, responsible fathering means being actively involved in the life of your child and taking a personal interest in your child's day-to-day joys and challenges. It means making a commitment to seek out, learn, and use the skills necessary to nurture your child's growth and development. It means staying connected to your child as she or he enters adolescence and adulthood. In short, it means putting your child first."

6. *Oxford English Dictionary* (Oxford: Clarendon Press); 2nd edition (New York: Oxford University Press, 1989), 1322.

7. "Beget" is defined in the *OED* as follows: "1. To get, to acquire (usually by effort). 2. To procreate, to generate: usually said of the father, but sometimes of both parents."

8. *Oxford English Dictionary* (Oxford: Clarendon Press); 2nd edition (New York: Oxford University Press, 1989), 968.

9. Ibid., 969.

10. Ibid.

11. Ibid., 1858.

12. Ibid.

13. Ibid., 969.

14. Ibid.

15. Ibid., 1858.

16. Ibid.

17. From "Me and All the Other Mothers," © 1988 Snowden Music.

18. Helen Schulman, " 'My Jim': Never the Twain, a Review of Nancy Rawles's Novel, *My Jim*," *New York Times Sunday Book Review,* January 30, 2005.

19. Quoted in Sarah Stewart Taylor, "Fatherhood Movement Has Range of Ideology, Agenda." Available at www.womensenews.org/article.cfm/dyn/aid/584/context/archive.

20. Susan Walzer, *Thinking about the Baby: Gender and Transitions into Parenthood* (Philadelphia: Temple University Press, 1998), 58.

21. Diane Ehrensaft, *Parenting Together: Men and Women Sharing the Care of Their Children* (Chicago: University of Illinois Press, 1990), 9.

22. Mr. Mom," Lonestar, Sony Music, 2004.

23. "The sky-god is a jealous god, of course. He requires total obedience from everyone on earth, as he is in place not for just one tribe but for all creation. Those who would reject him must be converted or killed for their own good. Ultimately, totalitarianism is the only sort of politics that can truly serve the sky-god's purpose." "America First? America Last? America at Last?" Lowell Lecture, Harvard University, 1992.

Chapter 3

1. To preserve the family's privacy, pseudonyms are used throughout this chapter.

2. She took progressively shorter leaves with each subsequent child because she had less (paid) leave time. She took about two and a half months for Elizabeth and six or seven weeks for Anthony.

3. In 1990, the company was acquired by the French multinational Saint-Gobain.

4. I suspect that accusations of molestation of children by men are overreported, that accusations of molestation by women are underreported, and that a broader range of physical interactions between women and children are seen as benign; still, the overall numbers are indisputable.

5. Ironically, in my own family, I've seen the flip side of this situation: When looking to hire a babysitter and a house cleaner, my sister refused to even consider hiring a man for either position; she wouldn't trust a man with her two daughters, and she didn't want to be alone in her house during the day with a man doing the cleaning.

6. I was able to look at records, for the ten-year period from 1996 to 2005, which detailed the composition of the board of directors and the group of people who chaired the various school committees every year. I looked at rough differ-

ences between the first five years and the second for the board and years two through five compared to the subsequent five for committee chairs (there were no committee chair data for 1996). In both areas, there was an increase in male participation between the two periods: from about 30 percent board membership up to 40 percent and from about 10 percent committee chairs up to 30 percent.

7. Quoted in Holly Leibowtiz Rossi, "Desperate Christian Housewives," Barnhill, available at www.beliefnet.com/story/155/story_15526_1.html.

Chapter 4

1. The opening section of this chapter appeared in slightly different form in Donald N. S. Unger, "Say Goodbye to Mr. Mom," *Worcester Magazine* (November 2005): 5.

2. The number 118 is a good number to use here: It's big, it's specific, and it gives an initial impression of being too ridiculously large to take seriously. But given his job—and the length of time he held it—Amory knew what he was talking about. The Web site tvdads.com lists well over 125 TV shows in which a single father (or father surrogate) figured prominently—and carries a warning label that the list is incomplete.

3. See www.tvdads.com.

4. He says this regarding issues of gender and power, in reference to the legal supposition that his wife acts only with his authorization.

5. This act, trumping race with humanity, is the moral core of the book. It has always infuriated me that the book has been both maligned and sometimes banned, tagged as racist for its use of (period-appropriate) language.

Chapter 5

1. The divorce rate in the United States, expressed as the annual number of divorces per thousand married women, went from 9.2 in 1960 to 22.6 in 1980. By the mid-1990s the rate had drifted downward slightly, to just under 20—still more than twice the rate in 1960. Tom W. Smith, "GSS Social Change Report No. 42: The Emerging 21st Century American Family," National Opinion Research Center, University of Chicago, November 24, 1999.

2. Quoted in Steve Beard, "Childhood Divorce Fuels Fire of New Rock," available at www.depressionisachoice.com/essays/childhood.htm.

3. Government statistics for the period from 2000 to 2004 show that fewer than 12 percent of infants in the United States were still breast-feeding at six months of age. "Breastfeeding Trends and Updated National Health Objectives for Exclusive Breastfeeding—United States, Birth Years 2000–2004," *MMWR* 56, no. 30 (August 2007): 760–763, available at www.cdc.gov/mmwr/preview/mmwrhtml/mm5630a2.htm.

4. I look briefly at the question of hormones in Chapter 7. One of the changes that take place, in both mothers and fathers, immediately before and after birth is a significant increase in the stress hormone cortisol, which is believed to impact parents by heightening vigilance and facilitating bonding with the newborn. As the phrase "*stress* hormone" might suggest, the chemical effect may be useful from an evolutionary point of view, but it is anything but calming.

5. "The word 'doula' comes from the ancient Greek meaning 'a woman who serves' and is now used to refer to a trained and experienced professional who provides continuous physical, emotional and informational support to the mother before, during and just after birth; or who provides emotional and practical support during the postpartum period." See www.dona.org/mothers/index.php.

Chapter 6

1. The books (and the setting) are British. The Disney movie, however, has deep American roots, which I expand on later in this chapter.

2. The analysis of *Mary Poppins* was first presented by this author in slightly different form, as "A Father Would Have to Be Crazy to *Mother*," at the Florida State University Literature and Film Conference in January 2000.

3. Refers to the archetypical "Introduction to Literary Criticism" required of English majors.

4. P. L. Travers, *Mary Poppins* (New York: Reynal and Hitchcock, 1934), 1.

5. Ibid., 2.

6. *Mary Poppins*, dir. Robert Stevenson, Disney, 1964.

7. Travers, *Mary Poppins*, 2.

8. The tape that has been used to repair the kite strongly resembles the Hebrew letter chet, which is the dominant letter in the word Chai, meaning "life" (the other letter, yod, looks like an apostrophe).

9. The analysis of *Kramer vs. Kramer* in this section was first presented by this author in slightly different form as "Ted Kramer and 'the *Other* Mothers'" at the Florida State University Literature and Film Conference in February 2001.

10. The marriage lasted thirty-seven years, until Judy Corman's death in 2004.

11. Michael Kernan, "Fathering of a Hit: 'Kramer' vs. Corman; Corman's 'Kramer'; The Author's Praise of Paternity," *Washington Post,* December 29, 1979, p. C1.

12. Quoted in Ibid.

13. In this section, unless otherwise specified, quotations and paraphrases of Jaffe, Benton, Hoffman, Streep, and Alexander are from the 2001 documentary *Finding the Truth: The Making of* Kramer vs. Kramer.

14. Hoffman and Byrne got divorced on October 6, 1980; Hoffman married Lisa Gottsengen on October 12, 1980, and they subsequently had four children together.

15. The clearest and most concrete measure of the depth of Hoffman's influence on the final script is the fact that Benton offered to share the screenwriting credit with him—Hoffman declined.

16. Jeff Lenburg, *Dustin Hoffman: Hollywood's Anti-hero* (New York: St. Martens Press, 1983), 145.

17. A cover sheet shown in the documentary lists the following: "1/6/78 Second Draft," "2/15/78 Revised Second Draft," "7/14/78 Revised Third Draft," "9/5/78 Revised Fourth (Final) Draft."

18. Available at http://rogerebert.suntimes.com/apps/pbcs.dll/article?AID=/19791201/REVIEWS/41004001/1023.

19. Available at www.blackpast.org/?q=primary/moynihan-report-1965 #chapter4. In chapter 4 of the report, entitled "The Tangle of Pathology," Moynihan writes in part, "In essence, the Negro community has been forced into a matriarchal structure which, because it is to [sic] out of line with the rest of the American society, seriously retards the progress of the group as a whole, and imposes a crushing burden on the Negro male and, in consequence, on a great many Negro women as well.

20. Statistics here and in the sections that follow are from the U.S. Census Bureau.

21. Worth noting, in this context, Moynihan wrote in the same section of the report, "But it may not be supposed that the Negro American community has not paid a fearful price for the incredible mistreatment to which it has been subjected over the past three centuries."

22. Regarding the marital status of such men, in 1968 (of a total of 8,332,000 children living with one parent), 178,000 children were living with a divorced father and 39,000 were living with a father who had never married. By 2006 (of a total of 20,619,000 children living with one parent), 1,495,000 were living with a divorced father and 1,255,000 were living with a father who had never married. This represents an increase in the percentage of children living with divorced fathers from 2.1 percent to 7.3 percent and an increase in the percentage of children living with never married fathers from less than 0.05 percent to just over 6.1 percent.

23. Kristin Helmore, "Raising a Child Alone: A Task More Men Are Seeking," *Christian Science Monitor*, March 25, 1985, p. 29.

24. Jamieson A. McKenzie, "Daddy's Little Girl, Up to Date," *New York Times*, February 26, 1989, p. 16.

25. "Two Unwed Women Strode toward Freedom but Somehow Got Lost," *People Weekly*, March 7, 1994, p. 49.

26. Sean Elder, "About Men: Dabbling Dads," *New York Times Sunday Magazine*, June 11, 1995, p. 30.

27. David Ray Papke, "Peace between the Sexes: Law and Gender in *Kramer vs. Kramer*," *University of San Francisco Law Review* (Summer 1996): 1199.

28. Rhymer Rigby, "Kramer vs. Kramer," *Management Today* (October 1998): 128.

29. Andrea C. Poe, "The Daddy Track," *HR Magazine* (July 1999): 79.

30. Radhika Chopra, "Retrieving the Father: Gender Studies, 'Father Love' and the Discourse of Mothering," *Women's Studies International Forum* 24, nos. 3–4 (May–August 2001): 445–455.

31. Michael Berry and Cäcilia Innreiter-Moser, "Communicating Cultural Dimensions of Gender-Related Identity in Female Austrian and Finnish Business Students' Responses to Joanna Kramer (and to Each Other)," *Culture and Organization* 8, no. 2 (2002): 161–189.

32. Torben Kragh Grodal, "Love and Desire in the Cinema," *Cinema Journal* 43, no. 2 (Winter 2004): 26–46.

33. In the revised third draft, from July 1978—at least four drafts were written—the text reads, "TED: (softly, but with real vehemence) Fuck you. He's my son. I'm staying with him."

34. What actually happens in custody cases is a hotly contested question. Both men and women argue that the system is skewed against them. U.S. Census Bureau statistics (2004) ascribe custody to the mother 83.1 percent and to the father 16.9 percent of the time. See www.census.gov/prod/2006pubs/p60-230.pdf. Men claim that this represents a bias against them in proceedings that are supposed to be gender neutral and hinge solely on "the best interests of the child." Women claim that, in the vast majority of cases, men do not contest custody and that, when they do, they are disproportionately successful. In contested cases, the father/mother, win/loss ratio is more or less 50/50—but that number is also "soft," at best. Child custody may be contested, by either parent, as a strategic move, sometimes with vindictive motivation. These cases are also more likely to involve more volatile household situations, on both sides.

35. Molly Haskell, "Hers," *New York Times*, February 11, 1982, p. C2.

Chapter 7

1. To preserve the family's privacy, pseudonyms are used throughout this chapter.

2. That gender is not crucial to bonding makes sense. The extreme example here—not merely cross-gender but cross-species—would be animal psychologist Konrad Lorenz's experiments in the 1930s, in which goslings bonded to *him* because he was the first thing they saw in their first hours of life.

3. The first search was completed in 2006; a follow-up was done in 2009.

4. Steve Craig, "Introduction: Considering Men and the Media," in *Men, Masculinity, and the Media*, ed. Steve Craig (Newbury Park, CA: Sage Publications, 1992), 2.

5. A. E. Storey, C. J. Walsh, R. Quinton, and K. E. Wynne-Edwards, "Hormonal Correlates of Paternal Responsiveness in New and Expectant Fathers," *Evolution and Human Behavior* 21 (2000): 79–95.

6. The trigger for these changes may be pheromones, odorless airborne chemicals that many species use to communicate about food, danger, or sex, among other things. The role of pheromones in human interaction is still a matter of some debate.

Chapter 8

1. Clea Simon, "Hooked on Advertising," *Ms. Magazine* (January 2001).

2. The analysis of this commercial was first presented by the author, in slightly different form, as "AT&T's *Reach Out* Commercials and the New American Family" at the Screen Media and Sexual Politics Conference at Plymouth State University, October 2004.

3. That last change might serve as an example of how flexibly we may interpret numbers. We can look at "soccer dad" increasing by a factor of ten and cite this as evidence that men are either more present "on the ground" or at least in public consciousness, in terms of their involvement with children. Or we can look at the fact that "soccer mom" still makes up almost 80 percent of the references and argue that, whatever has changed, four out of five of the references are still to women.

4. A June 2006 article in *BusinessWeek*, for example, cites a 2002 report from Mediamark Research that "shows that men were the principal purchaser of items like groceries and children's clothing in 21 percent of all US households" and notes that "this represents a rather large increase from 1985, where just 13 percent of men did most of the shopping."

5. A study produced by the Families and Work Institute—the 2003 National Study of the Changing Workforce—found that from 1977 through 2002, the amount of time that working mothers in dual-earner households spent caring for their children remained essentially the same; during the same period, the amount of time that men spent caring for their children almost doubled. The previously cited *BusinessWeek* article also notes that the "2005 US Census Bureau reports that only 98,000 men with children under 15 years old are in charge of the homestead, however the real number might be closer to two million, if one includes part-timers and freelancers who continue to generate some income while taking care of the kids at home."

Chapter 9

1. I spent a couple of days in Maryland talking to Kevin and his family in the summer of 2002. We got back in touch via e-mail in 2006, and I have integrated some of the updated information about his family situation that he provided at that time.

2. *Knussman v. Maryland*, Civil Action No. B-95-1255, U.S. District Court for the District of Maryland, Northern Division, Supplemental Complaint and Jury Demand, February 7, 1997, p. 5.

3. *Knussman vs. Maryland*, Appellate Brief. U.S. Court of Appeals for the 4th Circuit, October 3, 2000.

4. Albin Krebs and Robert McG. Thomas Jr., "Father's Leave Hinges on His Being Pregnant," *New York Times*, May 27, 1982, p. B15.

5. Francine M. Deutsch, *Halving It All: How Equally Shared Parenting Works* (Cambridge, Mass.: Harvard University Press, 1999), 181.

6. President Richard Nixon spent the bulk of his political career as an ardent anti-communist; ironically, the political capital this afforded him made it possible for his administration to open relations with communist China, in the early 1970s.

Epilogue

1. In 2003, the Families and Work Institute's "National Study of the Changing Workforce" reported a near doubling, between 1977 and 2002, of the amount of time that working fathers in dual-earner households spent caring for their children, while the amount of time working mothers devoted to child care remained essentially flat.

Appendix A

1. The 2009 search does something to demonstrate the instability of this kind of sampling. Isaac Asimov published a short story entitled "Feminine Intuition" in 1969. A group named the Music Machine (which subsequently became Bonniwell Music Machine) put out a song called "Masculine Intuition" in 1966; in 1996, the song was re-released in a cover version by Rocket from the Crypt. The 2009 "Feminine Intuition" search therefore excluded all hits that contained "Asimov." The 2009 "Masculine Intuition" search excluded all hits that contained "Music Machine," "Bonniwell," or "Rocket from the Crypt." Interestingly, this only seems to have made the division sharper, but it flags the complexity of extracting meaningful and credible numbers nonetheless.

Selected Bibliography

· · · · · · · · ·

Amory, Cleveland. *TV Guide* review of "The Courtship of Eddie's Father," 1969. Available at www.tvguide.com/news/Question-66860.aspx.

Angwin, Julia."Md. Trooper Joins Clinton Radio Show." *Baltimore Sun*, August 6, 1995, p. 8A.

Berlin, Isaiah. *Four Essays on Liberty*. London: Oxford University Press, 1969.

Bianchi, Suzanne M. "New Realities of Working Families: Overview." Paper presented at the Economic Policy Institute symposium, June 15, 1999. Available at www.dol.gov/dol/asp/public/futurework/conference/workingfamilies/work ingfamilies_toc.htm.

Cameron, Deborah, ed. *The Feminist Critique of Language: A Reader*. London: Routledge, 1990.

Campbell, Bebe Moore. *Successful Women, Angry Men*. New York: Random House, 1986.

Chandler, Daniel. *The Act of Writing*. Aberystwyth: University of Wales, 1995.

Chao, John. "Gender-Free Pronoun FAQ." February 14, 1996. Available at www .lumina.net/OLD/gfp/#hist.

Chapin, Harry. "Cat's in the Cradle." *Verities and Balderdash*. Compact disk. Elektra 1012. August 1974.

Cockey, Robin R. Letter to Walter E. Black, Jr., Senior Judge, U.S. District Court, District of Maryland. February 11, 1999. Available at www.aclu.org/news/ 1999/n021799c.html.

Corman, Avery. *Kramer versus Kramer*. New York: Random House, 1977.

Crawford, Mary. *Talking Difference: On Gender and Language*. London: Sage, 1995.

Crystal, David. *The Cambridge Encyclopedia of Language.* Cambridge: Cambridge University Press, 1987.

Deutsch, Francine M. *Halving It All: How Equally Shared Parenting Works.* Cambridge, Mass.: Harvard University Press, 1999.

Ehrenreich, Barbara. "The Politics of Talking in Couples." *Ms. Magazine,* May 1981, pp. 46–48.

Ehrensaft, Diane. *Parenting Together: Men and Women Sharing the Care of Their Children.* Chicago: University of Illinois Press, 1990.

Elder, Sean. "About Men: Dabbling Dads." *New York Times Sunday Magazine,* June 11, 1995, p. 30.

Epps, Garrett. "Dad's School-Time Jitters: Kindergarten Is the First Day of the Rest of My Son's Life." *Washington Post,* August 39, 1987, p. C5.

———. "It's De-witching Hour: After Two Decades as New Men, We Say the Devil with It." *Washington Post,* June 28, 1987, p. C5.

Fairclough, Norman. *Discourse and Social Change.* Cambridge, England: Polity Press, 1992.

Faludi, Susan. *Backlash: The Undeclared War against American Women.* New York: Crown, 1991.

———. *Stiffed: The Betrayal of the American Man.* New York: William Morrow, 1999.

Family and Medical Leave Act, Public Law 103-3, February 5, 1993.

"Fighting the Force: Denied Leave to Care for His Wife and Baby, a State Trooper Sues Maryland and Wins." *People Weekly,* March 1, 1999, p. 58.

Friedan, Betty. *Beyond Gender: The New Politics of Work and Family.* Washington, D.C.: Woodrow Wilson Center Press, 1997.

———. *The Feminine Mystique.* New York: W.W. Norton, 1963.

Gallagher, Maggie. "Peace Talks over the Housework Wars." *Sacramento Bee,* April 21, 1999, p. B9.

Gary, Sandra. "What Are We Talking About?" *Ms. Magazine,* December 1972, p. 73.

Geertz, Clifford. *The Interpretation of Cultures.* New York: Basic Books, 1973.

Gibaldi, Joseph. *MLA Handbook for Writers of Research Papers.* 5th ed. New York: Modern Language Association of America, 1999.

Gilligan, Carol. *In a Different Voice.* Cambridge, Mass.: Harvard University Press, 1982.

Gladwell, Malcolm. *The Tipping Point: How Little Things Can Make a Big Difference.* Boston: Little, Brown, 2000.

Gordon, Linda. "Functions of the Family." *WOMEN: A Journal of Liberation* (Fall 1969).

Grenier, Robert. "Movie Reviews." *Commentary* (November 1981): 86.

Handly, Donna, Deborah Harkins, Elizabeth Hemmerdinger, Janet Lynch, Wendy Marcus Raymont, Karen Rutledge. "What's a Ms.?" Preview issue. *Ms. Magazine,* Spring 1972, p. 4.

Harrison, Barbara Grizzuti. " 'Kramer vs. Kramer': Madonna, Child, and Mensch; Is It Different When All the Mother-Child Everyday Things Happen to a Father?" *Ms. Magazine,* January 1980, p. 30.

Haskell, Molly. "Hers." *New York Times,* February 11, 1982, p. C2.

Hatch, Robert. "Films." *The Nation,* January 26, 1980, p. 90.

Hays, Sharon. *The Cultural Contradictions of Motherhood.* New Haven, Conn.: Yale University Press, 1998.

Helmore, Kristin. "Raising a Child Alone: A Task More Men Are Seeking." *Christian Science Monitor,* March 25, 1985, p. 29.

Hochschild, Arlie Russell. *The Time Bind.* New York: Henry Holt, 1997.

———. "Time for Change." *Ms. Magazine,* September/October 1997, p. 39.

———. "Time in the Balance." *The Nation,* May 26, 1997, pp. 11–12.

Holoweiko, Mark. Letter. *New York Times,* March 11, 1982, p. C-13.

"I'd Rather Be with a Real Man™ Any Day!" 1997. Available at www.io.com/~wwwave/men/real.html.

Irving, John. *The World According to Garp.* New York: Random House, 1978.

Isele, Elizabeth. "Casey Miller and Kate Swift: Women Who Dared to Disturb the Lexicon." *WILLA* 3 (1994): 8–10.

Kaeser, Gigi. *Love Makes a Family: Portraits of Lesbian, Gay, Bisexual, and Transgender Parents and Their Families.* Amherst: University of Massachusetts Press, 1999.

Kanfer, Stefan. "Sispeak: A Msguided Attempt to Change Herstory." *Time Magazine,* October 23, 1972, p. 79.

Kelly, Joan B. "The Determination of Child Custody in the USA." Undated. Available at www.wwlia.org/us-cus.htm.

Kernan, Michael. "Fathering of a Hit: 'Kramer' vs. Corman; Corman's 'Kramer'; The Author's Praise of Paternity." *Washington Post,* December 29, 1979, p. C1.

King, Martin Luther, Jr. *I Have a Dream: A Speech in Defense of Freedom and Justice for All.* Rochester, N.Y.: Press of the Good Mountain, 1968.

Kleiman, Carol. "Equality at Home Can Be a Real Chore." *Ottawa Citizen,* September 23, 1998, p. H-4.

Knussman, Kevin. E-mail to the author. June 6, 2001.

Knussman vs. Maryland, Appellate Brief. U.S. Court of Appeals for the 4th Circuit. October 3, 2000.

Kramer vs. Kramer. Dir. Robert Benson. Warner Brothers, 1979.

Krebs, Albin, and Robert McG. Thomas, Jr. "Father's Leave Hinges on His Being Pregnant." *New York Times,* May 27, 1982, p. B15.

Krier, Beth Ann. "A Real Man Takes Aim at 80's Dating." *Los Angeles Times,* November 27, 1986, p. 5B-1.

Kübler-Ross, Elisabeth. *On Death and Dying.* New York: Macmillan, 1969.

Kuhn, Thomas S. *The Structure of Scientific Revolutions.* Chicago: University of Chicago Press, 1962.

Lakoff, Robin. *Language and Woman's Place.* New York: Colophon Books, 1975.

Leibman, Nina. "My Three Sons: U.S. Domestic Comedy." Undated. Available at www.mbcnet.org/ETV/M/htmlM/mythreesons/mythreesons.htm.

Lewin, Tamar. "Is Social Stability Subverted If You Answer 'I Don't'? Fears for Children's Well-Being Complicate a Debate over Marriage." *New York Times,* November 4, 2000, p. B-11.

Lewis, Oscar. *The Children of Sánchez.* New York: Random House, 1961.

Lorde, Audre. *Sister Outsider: Essays and Speeches.* Trumansburg, N.Y.: Crossing Press, 1984.

Lynch, Aaron. *Thought Contagion: How Belief Spreads through Society: The New Science of Memes.* New York: Basic Books, 1996.

Mann, Judy. "Woman's Way." *Washington Post,* December 21, 1983, p. B1.

Manning-Schaffel, Vivian. "Ads See Dad as Domestic Diva: Gender Roles Are Changing and Marketers of Household and Domestic Products Are Beginning to Target Men." *BusinessWeek,* June 16, 2006.

"Marketing 2000: An Assortment of Data and Observations That Will Impact Your Business." 4, no. 2 (Summer 1999). Available at www.meredithim.com/community/newsletter/closer.html.

Mary Poppins. Dir. Robert Stevenson. Disney, 1964.

McCartney, Bill. "Transcript: November 2000." Available at www.4thandgoal.org.

McKenzie, Jamieson A. "Daddy's Little Girl, Up to Date." *New York Times,* February 26, 1989, p. 16.

"Mending Broken Families." Editorial. *New Republic,* March 17, 1986, p. 7.

"Men Doing Their Share." Editorial. *Christian Science Monitor,* April 17, 1998.

Meyer, Eugene L. "Md. Trooper Alleges Sex Discrimination in Suit over Family Leave." *Washington Post,* April 29, 1995, p. B-03.

Milk, Leslie. "Macho, or All Other Things Being Equal." *Washington Post,* September 8, 1982, p. VA-2.

Miller, Casey, and Kate Swift. "De-sexing the English Language." *Ms. Magazine,* Spring 1972, p. 7.

———. *The Handbook of Nonsexist Writing for Editors and Speakers.* New York: Lippincott and Crowell, 1980.

———. *Words and Women.* New York: Anchor Press/Doubleday, 1976.

Miller, Casey, Kate Swift, and Rosalie Maggio. "Liberating Language." *Ms. Magazine,* September/October 1997, pp. 50–54.

Miller, Mark Crispin. "Getting Dirty." In *Boxed In: The Culture of TV.* Evanston, Ill.: Northwestern University Press, 1988.

Morgan, Robin, ed. *Sisterhood Is Powerful: An Anthology of Writings from the Women's Liberation Movement.* New York: Random House, 1970.

"Mother Returns Missing Boy." *Star Tribune* (Minneapolis), October 10, 1991, p. 2B.

Nieto, Ángel. *El Machinchar: Diálogo en Dos Voces.* New York: Scholastic, 1993.

Olin Hill, Alette. *Mother Tongue, Father Time: A Decade of Linguistic Revolt.* Bloomington: University of Indiana Press, 1986.

Oxford English Dictionary. 2nd ed. Oxford: Clarendon Press; New York: Oxford University Press, 1989.

Papke, David Ray. "Peace between the Sexes: Law and Gender in *Kramer vs. Kramer.*" *University of San Francisco Law Review* (Summer 1996): 1199.

Parsons, Talcott. *The Social System.* New York: Free Press, 1951.

Pekkanen, Sarah. "Catching Up with . . . Kevin Knussman. The Good Father Is a Good Mother: The State Trooper Who Sued for a Leave to Care for His Ill Wife and Baby Has Now Retired from the Force to Become a Full-Time Dad." *Baltimore Sun,* January 9, 2000, p. 3F.

Perry, Linda A. M., Lynn H. Turner, and Helen M. Sterk, eds. *Constructing and Reconstructing Gender: The Links among Communication, Language, and Gender.* Albany: State University of New York Press, 1992.

Plato. *The Dialogues of Plato.* Trans. B. Jowett. New York: Random House, 1937.

Poe, Andrea C. "The Daddy Track." *HR Magazine,* July 1999, p. 79.

Rankin, Deborah. "Personal Finance: Helping Parents Plan Their Finances." *New York Times*, August 4, 1985, p. C9.

Raphael, Sidney. Letter. *New York Times*, May 9, 1983, p. A-18.

Redfern, Jenny R. "Writing with Gender-Fair Language: The Generic He/Man Problem." Undated. Available at www.rpi.edu/dept/llc/writecenter/web/text/gender.html.

Rigby, Rhymer. "Kramer vs. Kramer." *Management Today* (October 1998): 128.

Rossi, Alice. *The Feminist Papers: From Adams to de Beauvoir.* New York: Columbia University Press, 1973.

Rubin, Donald L., and Kathryn L. Greene. "Effects of Biological and Psychological Gender, Age Cohort, and Interviewer Gender on Attitudes toward Gender Inclusive/Exclusive Language." *Sex Roles: A Journal of Research* 24, nos. 7–8 (April 1991): 391–412

Rubin, Lillian. *Intimate Strangers.* New York: Harper and Row, 1993.

Rybczynski, Witold. *Home: A Short History of an Idea.* New York: Penguin Books, 1986.

Salholz, Eloise, with Mark Uehling. "The Book on Men's Studies." *Newsweek,* April 28, 1986, p. 79.

Saussure, Ferdinand de. *Course in General Linguistics.* New York: McGraw-Hill, 1966.

Sayers, Dorothy. *Unpopular Opinions.* New York: Harcourt, Brace, 1947.

Schlesinger, Arthur, Jr. "The Movies: Growing Pains." *Saturday Review*, March 1, 1980, p. 34.

Schneir, Miriam. *Feminism: The Essential Historical Writings.* New York: Random House, 1972.

Schulman, Helen. "'My Jim': Never the Twain, a Review of Nancy Rawles's Novel, *My Jim.*" *New York Times Sunday Book Review,* January 30, 2005, p. 26.

Seeger, Pete, and Lee Hays. "If I Had a Hammer." Smithsonian/Folkways: SF CD 40062, 1996.

Seligmann, Jean, and Pamela Abramson. "Crack Pushes Dads to Duty." *Newsweek*, April 17, 1989, p. 64.

Seligmann, Jean, Debra Rosenberg, Pat Wingert, Hannah Dogen, and Peter Annin. "It's Not Like Mr. Mom." *Newsweek*, December 14, 1992, p. 70.

Siegel, Eric. "State Police Paramedic Who Won Suit over Denial of Parental Leave Retires." *Baltimore Sun*, July 8, 1999, p. B1.

Simon, Clea. "Hooked on Advertising." *Ms. Magazine*, January 2001, p. 54.

Smith, Tom W. "GSS Social Change Report No. 42: The Emerging 21st Century American Family." National Opinion Research Center, University of Chicago, November 24, 1999.

Sontag, Susan. *Against Interpretation and Other Essays.* New York: Dell, 1966.

Spender, Dale. *Man Made Language.* London: Routledge and Kegan Paul, 1985.

Steinem, Gloria. *Outrageous Acts and Everyday Rebellions.* New York: Penguin Group, 1983.

———. "The Politics of Talking in Groups." *Ms. Magazine*, May 1981, p. 43.

———. "Revving Up for the Next Twenty Five Years." *Ms. Magazine*, September/October 1997, p. 83.

———. "The Stage Is Set." *Ms. Magazine*, July/August 1982, p. 77.

———. "The Way We Were—and Will Be." *Ms. Magazine*, December 1979, p. 60.

Stephens, Kate. *Workfellows in Social Progression.* New York: Sturgis and Walton, 1916.

Storey, A. E., C. J. Walsh, R. Quinton, and K. E. Wynne-Edwards. "Hormonal Correlates of Paternal Responsiveness in New and Expectant Fathers." *Evolution and Human Behavior* 21 (2000): 79–95.

Suplee, Curt. " 'Real' Writers Are Raking It In: A Quiche Is Still a Quiche, but Here's the Best-Selling Dessert." *Washington Post*, January 6, 1983, p. E1.

"They Call Them 'Mr. Mom': A Growing Number of Black Fathers Raise Daughters and Sons by Themselves." *Ebony*, June 1991, p. 52

Thomas, E., and J. S. Kunen. "Growing Pains at 40: As They Approach Mid-life, Baby Boomers Struggle to Have It All." *Time*, May 19, 1986, p. 79.

Traugott, Elizabeth Closs, and Mary Louise Pratt. *Linguistics for Students of Literature.* San Diego: Harcourt Brace Jovanovich, 1980.

Travers, P. L. *Mary Poppins.* New York: Reynal and Hitchcock, 1934.

"Two Unwed Women Strode toward Freedom but Somehow Got Lost." *People Weekly*, March 7, 1994, p. 49.

Unger, Donald N. S. "Across the Florida Straits." *WFCR-FM*, Amherst NPR affiliate, January 26, 2000.

———. "AT&T's *Reach Out* Commercials and the New American Family." Screen Media and Sexual Politics Conference, Plymouth State University, October 2004.

———. "Changing Tables in Men's Rooms." *WFCR-FM*, Amherst NPR affiliate, December 28, 1998.

———. "The Christmas Tree Dilemma." *WFCR-FM*, Amherst NPR affiliate, December 15, 1999.

———. "Educational Accountability." *WFCR-FM,* Amherst NPR affiliate, December 12, 2001.

———. "Educational Success." *WFCR-FM,* Amherst NPR affiliate, September 28, 1999.

———. "A Father Would Have to Be Crazy to *Mother.*" Florida State University Literature and Film Conference, January 2000.

———. "Grow Up." *Worcester Magazine,* August 8, 1997, p. 7.

———. "The Invisible Man: The Gendering of Domestic Labor in Student Writing." Conference on College Composition and Communication, Atlanta, Georgia, March 1999.

———. "Killer in the Mirror." *WFCR-FM,* Amherst NPR affiliate, May 18, 1999.

———. "Kindergarten Drop Out." *WFCR-FM,* Amherst NPR affiliate, December 12, 2000.

———. "Making the Team." *WFCR-FM,* Amherst NPR affiliate, January 9, 2002.

———. "Outing Working Parents." *WFCR-FM,* Amherst NPR affiliate, February 12, 1999.

———. "Say Goodbye to Mr. Mom." *Worcester Magazine,* November 17, 2005, p. 5.

———. "Saying 'No' to Abstinence Education." *WFCR-FM,* Amherst NPR affiliate, October 12, 1998.

———. "Talking Back to Barbie." *WFCR-FM,* Amherst NPR affiliate, November 26, 1999.

———. "Ted Kramer and 'the *Other* Mothers,'" Florida State University Literature and Film Conference, February 2001.

———. "Turning the (Changing) Tables." *Voice Male,* Spring 1999, p. 13.

———. "What We're Afraid Of." *WFCR-FM,* Amherst NPR affiliate, October 27, 1999.

———. "When Children Kill Children." *WFCR-FM,* Amherst NPR affiliate, April 13, 1998.

———. "When Fathers *Mother.*" *Voice Male,* Summer 2000, p. 15.

———. "Where Do the Children Play?" *WFCR-FM,* Amherst NPR affiliate, June 1, 1999.

———. "Why Men Don't Take Family Leave: Why They Might." Modern Language Association Annual Convention, December 2002.

"United States Public Opinion Polls on Same-Sex Marriages" Undated. Available at www.marriageequality.com/facts/polls.htm.

U.S. Bureau of the Census. "Households, by Type: 1940 to Present." Released December 11, 1998. Available at www.census.gov/population/socdemo/hh-fam/htabHH-1.txt.

U.S. Department of Education. "Title IX: 25 Years of Progress." U.S. Department of Education, Washington, D.C., June 1997.

U.S. National Center for Health Statistics. "Monthly Vital Statistics Report." 43, no. 9. Supplement. Centers for Disease Control, Atlanta, March 22, 1995.

Vidal, Gore. *Julian.* New York: Ballantine Books, 1964.

Wainwright, Loudon, III. "Me and All the Other Mothers" Silvertone Records. ORE CD 500, 1989.

Walzer, Susan. *Thinking about the Baby: Gender and Transitions into Parenthood.* Philadelphia: Temple University Press, 1998.

Weedon, Chris. *Feminist Practice and Poststructuralist Theory.* Cambridge, Mass.: Blackwell, 1987.

White, Cynthia. "Leslie Feinberg: Author, Activist, Warrior." *Lambda Publications* (June 1996). Available at www.suba.com/~outlines/june96/authorle.html.

Whorf, B. L. "Science and Linguistics." *Technology Review* 42, no. 6 (1940): 229–231, 247–248.

Whyte, William H. *The Organization Man.* New York: Doubleday, 1956.

Wilkinson, John. Letter. *Seattle Times*, April 27, 1990, p. A11.

Will, George. "Sexist Guidelines—and Reality." *Washington Post,* September 20, 1974, p. A-29.

Wilson, Sloan. *The Man in the Gray Flannel Suit.* New York: Simon and Schuster, 1955.

"Working Wives, Threatened Husbands." Interview with Bebe Moore Campbell. *U.S. News and World Report*, February 23, 1987, p. 46.

Index

Donald N. S. Unger is a Lecturer in the Program in Writing and Humanistic Studies at MIT.